EYES ON GOD

FINDING HOPE IN THE NATURE OF GOD

Martin Springer

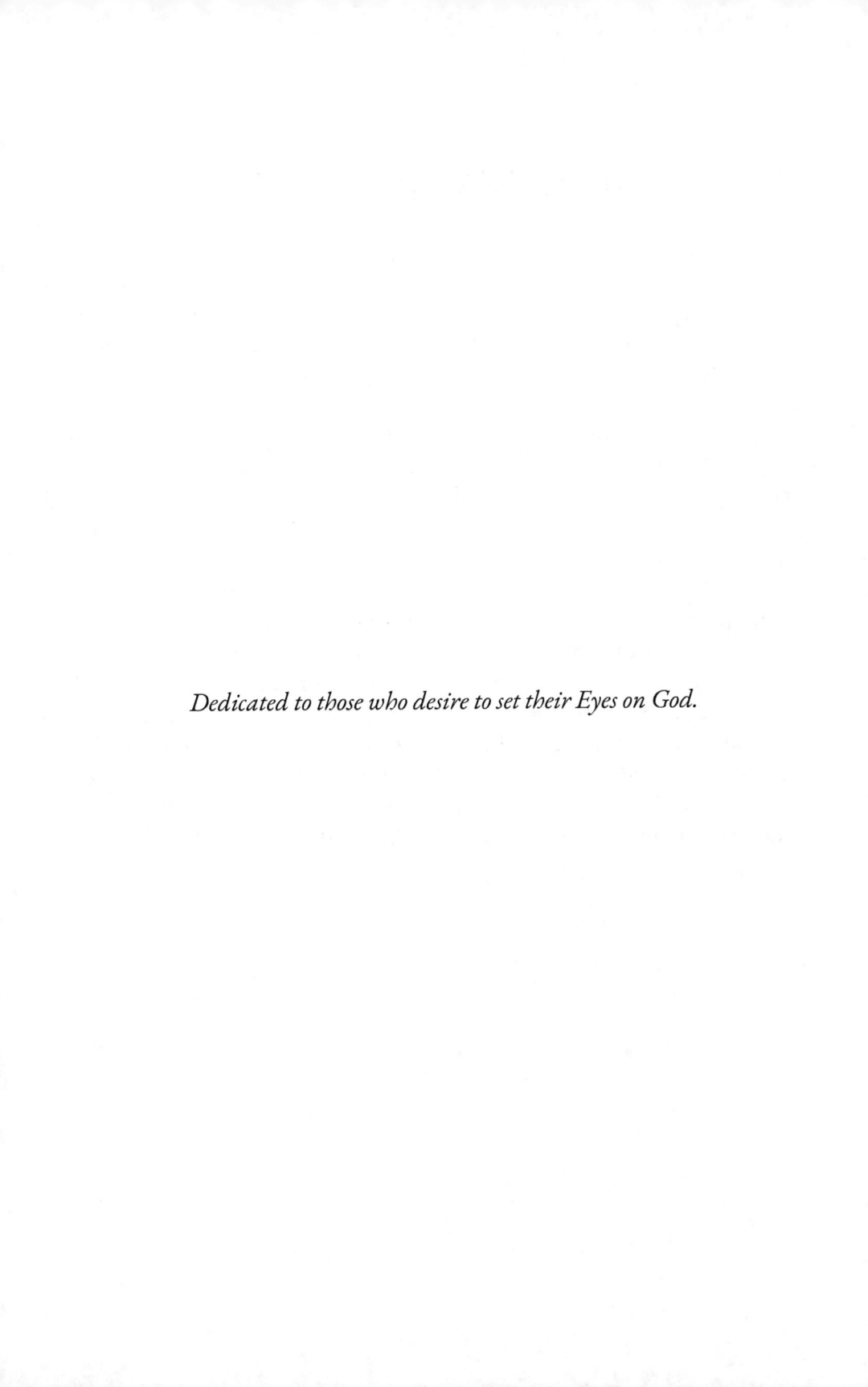

Dedicated to those who desire to set their Eyes on God.

ACKNOWLEDGMENT

There are four men whom I would like to mention in the writing of this book. They patiently listened to my concerns about Biblical passages that seem out of sync with God's revealed nature in scripture. I found these concerns too daunting to just gloss over. These men allowed me to raise serious questions about the nature of God and Christian doctrine. Their names are Chris Humphrey (Elder at Maranatha Bible Church in Springfield, Ohio), Tony Livigni (Pastor at Grace Church in Medina, Ohio), Steve Yoder (Superintendent of Kingsway Christian School in Orrville, Ohio) and Bob Collins (Pastor at Faith Baptist Church in Hartville, Ohio). They are a special breed of men, who reflect deeply on the meaning of scripture and recognize the limits to our human understanding. They are men who strive to ensure that their insights are fully aligned with scripture and the heart of God. They can discuss opposing ideas without growing defensive or argumentative. The result of these, sometimes challenging conversations, has always been edifying for me. I hope they would agree. These are four men that I respect and need in my life to ensure my thinking doesn't drift from sound hermeneutical principles. It is with a debt of gratitude that I acknowledge their influence on my life and in the writing of this book. Finally, any error in reasoning or understanding of a Biblical text that might be found in this book are solely my responsibility and should not be impugned on these four men.

TABLE OF CONTENTS

PREFACE

"You become like what you worship. When you gaze in awe, admiration, and wonder at something or someone, you begin to take on something of the character of the object of your worship."

N.T.Write

Those who make [idols] become like them; so do all who trust in them.

Ps 115:8 (ESV)

Anyone who professes to be religious has some concept of God in their thoughts. Their God may be something or someone they hold up as the ultimate standard to admire and imitate. Or He may be a God that terrifies them, and they cower in fear. Maybe He is simply an uninterested deity. Or He may be a God who loves them deeply if they please Him but will turn vindictive and harsh if they don't stay with His program.

The reality is whatever your concept of God happens to be, it is shaping who you are becoming as a person. In 1 Corinthians Paul tells followers of Christ they have a blurred concept of God. In one way or another, we all look at God through our humanness, which produces a fuzzy image of who He is and what He is like. Here are Paul's words in I Corinthians 13:12 (ESV):

"For now we see in a mirror dimly, but then face to face. Now I know in part; then I shall know fully, even as I have been fully known."

We have a problem. We are inclined to project our human nature onto God. It's easy to do, even when we study the Bible. This is probably unavoidable because our fallen human condition clouds our understanding. But it can do significant damage to our spiritual development so it is important to guard against it.

This book will talk about ways we compromise God's nature and discuss examples of how we unwittingly put boundaries on Him that are simply figments of our own imagination.

The main thesis I will be discussing is how to approach scripture and our relationship with God in a manner that can help us catch ourselves when we start to see God from a human perspective.

The methodology I'm using is similar to how counterfeit currency is identified. To recognize a counterfeit, you must first study the genuine thing carefully and in detail. You catch the fake because you know what the real thing looks like.

We will look intently at the nature of God as it is revealed in scripture. The goal is to strengthen our certainty about the essential aspects of His nature. Our assumptions and "logical" conclusions about God should never be in conflict with His revealed nature. Our faith in the nature of God is our greatest protection against false teaching. Any idea that violates, even in the slightest manner, what we know to be true about Him will cast a shadow of doubt in our minds. When this occurs, our faith has been compromised.

Reading this book may be more challenging than you think. All Christians hold assumptions about God that they believe to be scriptural, but actually, if true, they would be in conflict with His eternal nature. It takes a dose of humility along with a lot of patience and teachability to leave our comfort zone and enter into the boundless nature of God. It exposes our misconceptions and limitations. But I have found that the journey is well worth the discomfort. I invite you to walk with me through a few steps of this journey toward the heart of God.

It is from this place alone, with our eyes centered on God's heart, that we will begin to see our chaos and brokenness through His eyes. We will see our fallen world and our lost friends and family from His perspective.

May we all find hope in this life with our EYES FOCUSED ON HIM!

INTRODUCTION

What comes into our minds when we think about God is the most important thing about us.... Worship is pure or base as the worshipper entertains high or low thoughts of God. For this reason, the gravest question before the Church is always God Himself, and the most portentous fact about any man is not what he at a given time may say or do but what in his deep heart conceives God to be like.

A. W. Tozer

What is God really like? Do I worship Him as He truly is, or is He simply a concept I've created in my own imagination? It's a question I ask myself more frequently as the years race by. And I find that when I'm willing to challenge my concept of God, my love for Him grows much deeper. I hope I can find the words to express a few of the wonders that I have discovered.

I am not trying to write a theological thesis about the nature of God. People far more gifted than I have tackled that challenge. It's not that I don't enjoy good theology. I actually love it. But theology tends to focus more on academic resources and study techniques than it does on our relationship with God. It is the Spirit of God that ultimately leads us to the heart of God. Theology may help us better understand the scripture, but only the Spirit of God can draw us into a relationship with its author.

Nothing compares to knowing God. How we think and how we act are a direct reflection of what we believe about God. Any flaw in our concept of God will continue to be reflected in our character and manifest in our behavior. We end up imagining that God looks like us rather than becoming more like Him.

Shaping God into our image is the essence of idolatry.

Elevated thoughts of God produce an elevated living. Not the reverse. I first began to appreciate the significance of this principle, reflecting on John 14:21 (ESV): *"Whoever has my commandments and keeps them, he it is who loves me. And he who loves me will be loved by my Father, and I will love him and manifest myself to him."* Listen carefully. People who love God and desire to follow Him desperately need Jesus to reveal Himself to them. Why? It's the only way we will become like Him. Christlikeness is caught from Him by being with Him. We must silence all other voices and listen for His. The apostle John put it this way: *"We love because He first loved us"* (1 John 4:19 ESV). Love grows in me as I understand and experience more of His infinite Love. My love will never be greater than my understanding and experience of His love.

C. S. Lewis illustrates the idea in the following quote from Mere Christianity:

"If you want to get warm you must stand near the fire: if you want to be wet you must get into the water. If you want joy, power, peace, and eternal life, you must get close to, or even into, the thing that has them. They are not a sort of prize which God could, if He chose, hand out to anyone. They are a great fountain of energy and beauty spurting up at the very center of reality. If you are close to it, the spray will wet you: if you are not, you will remain dry. Once a man is united to God, how could he not live forever? Once a man is separated from God, what can he do but wither and die."

Knowing God is not the same thing as knowing the Bible and having good morals. The Christian faith is not primarily about knowing and doing the right things. It is about knowing God. For sure, it does produce good morals and right living. But what makes the Christian faith unique is that it changes the heart and brings an intimacy with our creator. It is allowing scripture to take us into the great mystery of our unseen God. The closer we grow toward seeing God for who He really is, the more we will desire to be like Him and the more genuine our worship becomes. This idea cannot be learned in an academic study of the Bible. It can only be known experientially through an unquenchable desire to know the heart of God.

For knowledgeable believers, it's important to answer the question: "Am I trusting God, or am I trusting my understanding of the Bible?". When Christians say they trust the Bible what they typically mean is they trust their understanding of the Bible. But when that understanding (theology) appears to be in conflict with the nature of God, are we willing to challenge our theology, or do we change our concept of God? The following is a simple illustration of the question:

Christians believe that Scripture teaches that God is sovereign over his creation, which He is (Eph. 1:11; Prov. 16:33; Job 42:2) and that He also has a deep desire for all men to come to repentance, which He does (I Tim 2:4; II Pet. 3:9). But many conclude God is unable to reach all mankind because He gave them "freedom of choice." I don't find this limitation of God actually taught in the Bible. It is the product of deductive reasoning, not divine revelation.

The reasoning goes like this - God does all that He can to reach as many as possible, but He has given mankind freedom of choice. This means, according to the logic, that it is ultimately mankind who has the final say in their salvation. And so God, because He is just, must subject the majority of mankind to suffer eternal judgment, all the while desiring a different outcome. Many who hold this view are uncomfortable with forthrightly proclaiming it, and rightly so. Why the discomfort? God's love has been thwarted by man's free will, and His justice must be satisfied. Justice wins, and His love is eternally frustrated. There is an eternal conflict within the nature of God. Forever, He must live with a longing in His heart for billions of people, helplessly watching them as victims of free will, which ironically is His own creation.

This is an example of how our reasoning can compromise the inner harmony of God's nature in an attempt to align it with the human concept of freedom of choice. My purpose is not to investigate a series of these challenges but to remind the reader that our faith should be solely in the author of scripture and not a system of theology.

The point I want to make now is that we must first be firmly established in our understanding of the nature of God and then recognize when our theology is in some way distorting our view of God. I believe this is a serious problem in Christian theology that is often not recognized or too easily dismissed. My hope in writing this is to shed some light on the problem.

In the following pages, I will probably challenge some of your thoughts about God. I got here by challenging my own ideas and it resulted in a rather significant change in the way I approach the Bible. I used to see the Bible through the lens of the systematic theology I had studied and come to believe. I had learned to interpret scripture and shape my understanding of God by bringing them into alignment with that theological framework.

The problems with this approach became increasingly evident over the years. The inconsistencies between the theology and the God I found being revealed in scripture became too problematic. While I still find systematic theology to be a valuable tool, I no longer consider it to be the primary filter as I approach scripture.

We all use filters to guide our thinking. They are the assumptions and convictions we believe to be true. We interpret all new input through these filters and try to align the new discoveries to that framework. Filters aren't bad. They help us make sense out of the chaos in this world.

It's inevitable that we will use filters as we approach scripture, and the longer we've been Christians the more powerful those filters become. When we hear something that significantly challenges that filter we quickly respond by looking for a way to protect the filter. For most mature Christians, the primary filter is the theological framework they have been taught. We continually interpret the Bible through that lens. When we read something in Scripture that seems in conflict with our theology, we seek a way to bring it into alignment. We should be on the alert when we are doing this.

Good theology is important, but it is not the goal when we study scripture. The Bible is God's self-revelation to us. (Genesis 16:13; 17:1; 28:12,13; Exodus 3:14; Matthew 11:27; II Corinthians 3:18) The purpose of scripture is knowing God for who He truly is. And that purpose is only fulfilled when the Spirit of God teaches us (I Corinthians 2:10-16), and the Son of God reveals the Father to us (Matthew 11:27; John 6:44; 14:6-10). When my theological framework is in conflict with the revealed nature of God, I need to be willing to challenge my theology and resist the temptation to adjust the nature of God to resolve the conflict.

A few paragraphs earlier, I stated that I no longer use a theological framework as my primary filter when reading the Bible. I still use theology as a secondary filter, but the nature of God, as revealed in scripture, has become my primary filter. As I read a passage, I ask myself, how does this align with what I know to be true about God's nature? And how does it allow me to see Him more clearly? If what I see appears to be in conflict with His essential nature, I will stop, pray and ask God to help me see Him more clearly in the passage I'm studying.

Knowing God, not theology, is the goal. Let me illustrate.

Romans 9:13 says: "...Jacob I loved but Esau I hated". We have a problem!!! If God is love, as scripture proclaims (I Jn 4:19), how can He hate Esau?

My **Theological filter concludes** – that hate must be a relative term, so I assume that God still loves Esau but He loves Jacob much more. The gap in his love for the two men is so great that His love for Esau is called hate when contrasted with His love for Jacob. And I conclude God doesn't love everyone with the same level of love. Doesn't that make sense? It fits my own personal experience of love. So, I'm willing to think God's love works the same way. But what I have done is project my human view of love onto God.

Stay with me. God is love, and love is never diminished in God. For God to be God, it is impossible that He hates Esau or loves him less. I don't dare walk away from this passage diminishing the love of God.

My **Nature of God filter concludes** - that God is perfect love, which is always and completely expressed in everything God does. He loves His entire creation, including each individual, with a perfect, pure, eternal love (this will be more fully developed later). However, while God does love everyone with the same love, He does not show that love in the same way. He choses how he will show that love, and He will always do it in a way that perfectly reflects all of His divine nature, including His love.

It's like a parent who loves all their children but treats them differently. Their love will be expressed in a way that is best for each child. One may be shown grace and the other punishment because that is what love discerned would be best.

Every action that God takes toward His creation will always reflect perfectly all aspects of His divine nature in all their fullness. His love, justice, righteousness, holiness etc., will be 100% manifest in all His actions. So God does not, cannot, hate Esau or love Him less than Jacob.

God is agape, which means perfect love (I Jn 4:16). If He ever responds in any way that is not fully motivated by agape, then the apostle John was wrong, and perfect agape love is not his eternal nature. In that case, we could not say God is agape (The section on God's Oneness will help explain this). And we end up with a God who chooses to love or not to love based on the circumstances.

My **theological filter** is willing to accept the idea that God is agape, but He doesn't always choose to demonstrate that kind of love. My **nature of God filter** says, "Agape is not a choice God makes. He is, always and forever, Agape."

He chooses how He will love, not if or how much He will love. If His eternal nature is agape, as scripture teaches, then there is never a time when God chooses not to demonstrate that agape.

To say that God had a lack of, or lesser form of, love for Esau is to tamper with His divine nature. It also diminishes my personal view of love and justifies an unloving attitude toward others that I don't particularly like. My theological filter has led me astray. So, I choose to keep meditating, praying and searching the scriptures for a better understanding.

Here's a resolution for this illustration. Jesus used a similar love/hate expression with His disciples when He said: _"If anyone comes to me and does not hate his own father and mother and wife and children and brothers and sisters, yes, and even his own life, he cannot be my disciple."_. (Luke 14:26 ESV)

On the other hand, Paul said that men _"should love their wives like Christ loved the church"_ (Ephesians 5:25 ESV). Is Paul contradicting Jesus? Of course not. Jesus' standard for love was always perfect "agape" love. And it is His example that we are to follow.

Jesus even taught us that to be His disciples, the character of our love for others was to be so perfect that it was a new commandment (_"A new commandment I give to you, that you love one another: just as I have loved you, you also are to love one another. By this all people will know that you are my disciples, if you have love for one another."_ John 13:34,35 ESV). The new commandment is to love others with God's infinite unfailing love, not just human love. Jesus was saying, "watch me love, and then you love each other like that."

OK, fine, but why did Jesus use all the "hate speech" in Luke 14:26? The love/ hate contrast appears to be an ancient idiom meaning to make a choice.

Jesus was saying you must choose me over every human relationship if you want to be my disciple. And if you make that choice, the nature and extent of your love for them will increase. In the Romans 9 passage Paul was saying that God chose Jacob, not Esau, to be in the lineage of the messiah. It has nothing to do with His level of love for the two brothers. He loves them both with a perfect enduring love because God is love.

If you find yourself concluding that God chooses some to love with a perfect "agape" love, but he has some lower love for the rest of mankind, you are drawing a conclusion that the Bible never teaches. You've made an assumption about God's nature to fit your theological understanding.

My motivation in writing this is not to challenge anyone's theology. I am inviting you to read the scriptures, looking for the heart of God rather than aligning it to a theological conviction. I'd like to encourage you to be certain you know who God actually is, as revealed in scripture, and then guard that understanding as you read through the pages of the Bible.

An unbelieving friend of mine recently asked me if I believed both the new and old testaments of the Bible. I said, "Yes, but why do you ask?". He explained that he viewed the Old Testament God as harsh and the New Testament Jesus as kind and gracious. How can they be the same God? It's a tough question, but it perfectly illustrates the point I'm making.

When we shape our understanding of God's nature by looking at His actions, we will develop a shallow, human-like understanding of His character. But when we shape our understanding of His actions by looking at His nature it will elevate our understanding of His character. God is not bipolar, motivated by love in the New Testament and by justice in the Old. We should never project that kind of human flaw onto the nature of God.

There is a great story in the book of Luke that describes two disciples walking together and having a conversation. They are trying to understand the scriptures and the events they have just witnessed from a human perspective. The story is known as the Disciples on the road to Emmaus (Luke 24:13-35).

The resurrected Christ joined them as they walked down the road, discussing the reports they had heard about His resurrection. Their eyes did not recognize that it was him. He listened to them in all their confusion and then finally began to speak:

And he said to them, "O foolish ones, and slow of heart to believe all that the prophets have spoken! Was it not necessary that the Christ should suffer these things and enter into his glory?" And beginning with Moses and all the Prophets, **he interpreted to them in all the Scriptures the things concerning himself.** *(Luke 24:25-27 ESV)*

Jesus revealed Himself to them in the Old Testament. They couldn't see Him in the pages of scripture until He showed them. The same is true for us.

As the story progresses, the disciples do not recognize Jesus until later at the dinner table. Their eyes were opened, and when they recognized Him, He vanished from their sight. They said to each other, *"Did not our hearts burn within us while he talked to us on the road, while he opened to us the Scriptures?"* (Luke 24:32 ESV)

Just like these two disciples, we need Jesus to open our eyes to see Him throughout the pages of scripture. The Bible is God's self-revelation, and we go there to see Him. If He doesn't join us on our journey down life's road we also will remain in confusion. We need Him to interpret to us in all the scripture the things concerning Himself.

My prayer is that you might find your heart burning within you as He reveals Himself to you from the pages of scripture.

SECTION 1 - GOD'S CHARACTER VS HIS ACTIONS

"..., for out of the abundance of the heart, his mouth speaks.".

Luke 6:45 (ESV)

Being always precedes doing!

This is not only true for the human race. It is also true about God. God's actions always flow out of His nature. And if we lose sight of this, our understanding of God becomes distorted.

With this in mind, we'll start by focusing on the distinction between who God is (His essential attributes or character) and what God does (His temporal actions). God's actions can be seen in creation, but His nature is transcendent. It exists apart from creation. Understanding this distinction can have a significant impact on our concept of and relationship with God, as I've learned through personal experience. In this section I will try to bring more clarity to this distinction and explain its importance.

God's eternal essence is who He is outside of creation, outside of time and space. It consists of those things that are true about God's nature independent of any creative act on His part. These attributes define the very essence of God, His eternal nature, apart from His interaction with creation.

God's interactions with creation are temporal in nature and can change as the circumstances change. The Bible even describes God as occasionally changing His mind (Ex. 32:14, Jer. 26:19, Jonah 4:2). His wrath can shift into forgiveness, and His mercy can turn to judgment, and yet his nature never changes. His responses to creation should never be confused with His unchanging, eternal nature. These actions do not define His nature, but they will always perfectly reflect it.

Scripture does give us some insight into the essential attributes of God that describe His nature outside of any interaction with His creation. I will be focusing on 9 of these, which include:

1. God is Self-Existent
2. God is Holy
3. God is One
4. God is Eternal
5. God is Immutable
6. God is Relational
7. God is Love
8. God is Righteous and Just
9. God is Without Limits

All of these attributes are present in God apart from the time/space/matter creation. They are separate from creation. They are revealed in scripture to help us understand the perfect, eternal essence of God as He exists apart from His creation.

There are also actions that God takes within His creation that are, inappropriately, in my judgment, often referred to as attributes of God by many writers. They include actions such as His anger, wrath, forgiveness, grace and mercy. These are temporal expressions that reflect all aspects of His unified eternal nature, but they only exist in the context of a fallen creation. Let me explain.

When we refer to God as gracious, merciful and forgiving or as vengeful and wrathful, we are referring to his responses to a fallen human race. These words describe God's response within creation to varying circumstances. They are attributes of His behavior but they are not an aspect of His unchanging nature. These behavioral attributes shift as circumstances change. God's nature never shifts in any way.

So why am I stressing this idea so strongly?

Because confusion between the attributes of God's character and the attributes of His behavior can lead to errors in our understanding of the nature of God. And the further we drift from a pure understanding of God's eternal nature, the closer we are to creating a God in our own image. Yes, it is that important!

In this section, I want to introduce my misconceptions about God's nature. And I believe these misconceptions are rather pervasive among Christians. Let me begin to explain by looking at a few chapter titles from the table of contents in Arthur Pink's Classic on the Attributes of God:

The Immutability of God
The Holiness of God
The Knowledge of God
The Power of God
The Love of God
The Grace of God
The Mercy of God
The Wrath of God

There is an important difference between the first five chapters and the last three. The first five describe the nature of God and help us understand His character.

They describe who God is independent of creation.

The last three are examples of God's interaction with the fallen human race. They are attributes of God's behavior, and they change as the circumstances change. Grace (undeserved favor), Mercy (Patiently waiting for repentance), and Wrath (anger toward sin) are God's responses to sin. They are not attributes of the nature of God. They are actions describing how God responds to sin and they vary depending on the circumstances.

God's actions vary and change based on the circumstances. But His nature never changes. As we reflect on the chapters discussing His Oneness and His Immutability, we are assured that His nature perfectly, eternally, unwaveringly and without exception is fixed. Under no circumstance will His nature ever vary!

In Pink's Table of Contents he includes both the attributes of God's eternal character and His actions within creation as chapters describing the attributes of God's nature. This is confusing. It blurs the distinction between God's unchanging character and His actions that change as circumstances change.

We should always maintain a clear distinction between God's nature and His actions in our thinking. Failure to do so can quickly muddle our understanding of God's character.

God's nature or character does not vary. It is unchangeable. God's love and His justice will never shift. But God's mercy can shift to wrath because they are both His responses to creation. His actions are always directed by His nature,

18

but they vary and change as circumstances change. Unfortunately, this distinction is often ignored.

Let me illustrate how this happens: I did a Google search on questions about "God's wrath vs. God's love". Here are a few of the questions returned:

1. Is there a contradiction between God's love and wrath?

2. How can God be love and wrath at the same time?

3. How can a God of love also be a God of wrath?

4. We talk a lot about God's love and grace, but what about His wrath and anger?

These questions are confusing. They blur the distinction between God's nature and His actions. How can God be a God of love and a God of wrath? Let's begin to unwrap this.

Notice the 4 "attributes" that are referenced in the various questions: Love, Grace, Wrath and Anger. Love defines an aspect of God's character. His nature is love (I John 4:8). Grace, wrath and anger describe actions God chooses to take as the circumstances vary. Wrath is not a character trait; it is an action of God. God is love. He is always unchanging, never diminishing love. It is an eternal aspect of His character. When He demonstrates wrath, it is always an expression of His character, which includes His love. God is love. He is not wrath. In fact, in the chapter on God's love, we will see how God's anger is actually an aspect of His love.

When we see God doing things in scripture that we don't understand, such as His command to Saul to slaughter all the Amalekite men, women, children, and even babies along with the live stock (I Samuel 15:1-3), we may be tempted to think of God as harsh and even vindictive. After all, it was God who instructed Saul to slaughter even the babies. How could a God of love do such a thing? One response that is frequently offered to explain this problem is: "you have to remember that God is not only love but also just." What does that even mean? Are there situations when His justice takes priority over His love? Is that what God is really like? And we are left with confusion and doubt about who God really is. The purpose of this book is to provide an approach to reading scripture that helps us process this confusion. I hope the reader finds it helpful.

Listen carefully. We cannot understand who God is by observing the circumstances of this world. That approach inevitably leads to the confusion and doubts about God's character that we saw in the last paragraph. In reality, the reverse is true. We begin to understand the circumstances of this world as we grow in our understanding of who God is. We do not look to the world to understand God. We look at God to understand the world. Paul expressed this idea to the church in Col. 3:2 (ESV), "Set your minds on things above, not on things that are on earth.". We begin to understand this world when we focus our minds on knowing its creator.

As we probe deeply into the essence of God's nature, we will begin to understand difficult passages like I Samuel 15 based on what we confidently know to be true about God. Toward the end of the book, I will return to this passage and discuss how we might align our understanding of I Sam. 15:1-3 to what we know to be true about God.

As this change in perspective began to take root in my mind it started to change the way I think about God and how I read the scriptures. I don't draw conclusions about what God is like by looking at what He does. I draw conclusions about what God does by looking at what He is like, by looking at His nature as revealed in scripture.

I have come to realize that this idea is much more important than I first imagined. I used to think of God's grace and mercy as His love in action and His anger and wrath as His justice in action. I thought this way without even realizing it. It is a flawed perspective.

Everything that God does fully and completely reflects all of His nature. It is not that some actions reflect a particular aspect of His nature and other actions a different aspect. As we will see in the nine chapters on God's nature, His every action reflects, without limit, the totality of His nature.

God is not defined by His actions. Being always precedes doing. Jesus said it this way - Out of the overflow of the heart, the mouth speaks (Luke 6:45). Our actions don't define our character, but they do reflect it. The same is true for God. The best way to understand anything is to look at the real thing, not a reflection of it. God's actions are a reflection. His nature is the real thing.

Both wrath and forgiveness are God's responses to sin. Only when sin, rebellion and corruption entered creation did these temporal actions become expressions by God. They reflect His nature. But referring to them as attributes distorts His nature. They do not define His eternal nature, but they always perfectly reflect the composite set of His essential attributes (love, holiness, justice etc). These temporal "attributes" are better described as actions of God in the temporal universe. While they only exist in the presence of sin and imperfection, they do serve God's eternal purpose by moving the entire universe forward toward complete reconciliation with God (II Cor. 5:19; Col. 1:20).

Every interaction God has with His creation is a temporal choice that He makes to fulfill His eternal purposes, and all of them are motivated by the fullness of His nature, including both His love and His justice. The unrepentant will experience God's love and justice in His wrath. The repentant will experience them in His forgiveness. Every temporal action God makes in creation is always a manifestation of everything He is.

This is wonderful news. God's judgments are perfect in every way. He has the power to fulfill all of His purposes. His actions are just, and all His choices perfectly reflect His righteousness and are motivated by His love. There are no exceptions when it comes to His eternal nature. All the doubts about God that we experience in our lives and ponder in our hearts should melt away. This is hope-producing, fear-destroying good news. Whenever you sense a shadow of doubt about the goodness of God creeping into your heart, turn back to Him so that He may restore your hope. The perfection of His eternal nature is your hope.

May we rediscover, or possibly discover for the first time, the untarnished beauty of our Creator.

SECTION 2 - GOD'S ESSENTIAL NATURE

Part 1 - God is Self-Existent
(Jn 8:24, Ex. 3:14)

Nothing comes from nothing. Nothing ever could...

Sound of Music

The idea of self-existence is beyond our comprehension. We see everything from the perspective of a cause-and-effect universe. Scientific theory relies on cause and effect to explain everything. But when science tries to explain the origins of the universe, it begins to self-destruct. Did it start with the big bang? Did it come from an infinitely dense singularity of matter? If so, where did the singularity come from? And thus, our attempt to understand is hijacked by the cause-and-effect nature of the universe.

The first cause in a cause-and-effect creation must originate outside of the universe. The first 4 words of the Bible make this idea very clear: _In the beginning GOD_ (Gen 1:1). Our origins cannot be known by science because science can only observe the creation itself. They can only be known if they are somehow revealed to us from some source outside of creation. It is when we realize this fact that we are ready to discover the self-existent one. The Bible calls him Yahweh or the great I AM.

People like to ask the question: "If God created the universe, who created God?". The answer, of course, is that God was not created. God just is. This does not mean that God has always existed. It's much more profound than that.

God is not bound by time. His existence is not governed by the laws of creation, including the ticking of a clock that defines the boundaries of our human lives. He created time and exists apart from time. To say that God has existed forever is to think of His existence in human terms. His self-existence is better described as timeless rather than forever.

God's self-existence can be a terrifying thought. It can also bring great comfort. He depends on nothing in this universe. Everything that does exist exists because of Him. The fact that anyone exists is because of His self-existence. The universe is totally dependent on His existence and will ultimately bow to His authority. This is terrible news if there is even the slightest flaw in God's character. But it is a great source of joy if God is infinitely and perfectly good.

So, asking the question, "who is God?" is the most important question we could ever ask. This is what motivates me to capture my thoughts on God's nature.

Our existence is completely reliant on His self-existence, and the quality of our existence depends on His self-existent nature. What I can confidently say is that there is not even the slightest possibility of a character flaw in God. That makes God's self-existence the greatest news we could ever hear. My hope is that reflecting on these insights into His nature will guide you deeper into His love for you and strengthen your confidence in His flawless beauty.

It is because of God's self-existence, apart from His creation, that the scripture proclaims that God is Holy. We will look at that next.

Part 2 - God Is Holy
(Is. 6:3; Hab. 1:3; Ex. 3:2,4-5; Heb. 12:29)

And they were calling out to one another: "Holy, holy, holy is the LORD of Hosts; all the earth is full of His glory."

Isaiah 6:3 (ESV)

The word Holy is the only attribute of God repeated three times in scripture to describe God. There are certainly many reasons for this, but I would like to focus on one. Both the Hebrew (Qadosh) and Greek (Hagios) words translated holy means separate or different from. When we say that God is Holy, it means that God is different and totally separate from HIS creation. It is important to understand the implications that His holiness has on all aspects of His nature.

God's essential nature exists apart from and independent of His creation. God is never to be defined in terms of the time/space/matter universe. He created matter and space, and he created time. But He should never be defined or limited by them. God's holiness is a refutation of all religions that worship some aspect of creation. It is a direct refutation of Pantheism, which teaches the universe as a whole is God. The Bible says no, God is Holy.

God is separate from and independent of His creation. He does interact with His creation in profound ways, but that interaction must always be understood in a way that is consistent with His essential nature apart from creation. We should never look at God's actions and draw conclusions about Him that compromise His revealed nature in scripture. To do so is a form of idolatry.

To put it another way, our tendency is to seek an understanding of God by reflecting on how he interacts with the fallen human race. We think about events we experience in this life and draw conclusions about God. When we do this, we inevitably use human reasoning to draw conclusions about God's essential nature.

A classic example goes something like this: "How can God be called love when good people suffer in this world?". Human reasoning concludes that God is either unloving and won't stop the suffering, or He lacks power and can't stop it, or possibly He has a greater plan that takes precedence over His love. I have an agnostic friend who firmly believes this logic irrefutably destroys any credibility to what the Bible says about God's love. My friend is trying to understand God by looking at the creation. He looks at the world's suffering and believes He sees a flaw in God's nature. But the injustice and suffering we experience in this life are not a reflection of some flaw in God's nature. They are a reflection of how sin has corrupted His goodness, as seen in creation. Creation is broken, not the creator. While the creation does point to God, it doesn't fully explain what God is like. Approaching an understanding of God's nature in this manner results is an idolatrous view of God based on human reason rather than God's self-revelation in the Bible.

The alternative is to understand the creation by looking at God. With this change in perspective, we interpret this world, along with all its pain, through the lens of God's Holy nature. His Holy nature is everything that God is outside of or apart from His creation. You can never begin to understand the insanity of this life until you start to see it through the lens of His Holy nature. I have referred to God's Holy nature as His essential nature throughout this discourse.

So, how do we make this change to our perspective? We reflect on who God is, as revealed in scripture, before we try to understand what God does. This principle is what sets us free to love God without reservations and to trust Him with no hesitation. It is the foundational principle of walking by faith. If we are tempted to reverse the order, we are trying to understand who God is from creation's perspective. Bad idea!! It inevitably leads to human error.

We must seek to understand creation by first focusing on God's essential nature. God is Holy and His existence is not dependent on, nor is it defined by what we observe in creation. Because God is Holy, we are dependent on His self-revelation to know what He is really like. Without the scripture to guide our understanding, we are all groping in the dark.

This is a good place for an example. The Bible teaches us that God is eternal. (Rom 1:20) If we think of this as meaning that God will live forever, we are trying to understand God from creation's perspective, and we violate His holiness.

Why? We are trying to understand God's eternal nature based on our concept of time. But our concept of time is a part of God's creation.

The fact that He is HOLY tells us He is separate from His creation. He is set apart from time. He is timeless. He has no beginning or end because those concepts only exist within HIS creation. He is ageless. He does not experience the passing of time. We experience life moment by moment. God is holy, which means He does not experience a linear progression of time like we do. A clear understanding of His holiness is a critical first step in avoiding confusion over His essential nature. And the only way we can know this about God is through His self-revelation in scripture and the illumination of our minds by His Spirit.

Understanding God's holiness is vital. I have struggled for years over the question: "what is God really like?". It has been reflecting on His holiness that transformed my thinking. His holiness is the source of our confidence in Him and why He can be trusted in everything. His nature is holy, separate, untouchable and incorruptible. To be Holy also means His nature is flawless and can never be improved.

Our relationships in this world depend on human nature. These relationships are damaged and frequently leave us broken and disappointed. But His nature is Holy, infinitely more than the best of human nature. If He were not Holy, we would have to wonder when His weakness would show up. Like superman, what is God's kryptonite? But He has no hidden weakness or vulnerability. We can trust Him without reservation because He is Holy. Retracted reflection on God's Holiness is the only way to direct our thoughts away from the temporal mindset of this world.

Consider how God's holiness is seen in the life and ministry of Jesus. He is our best and most tangible view of what God's holy nature is like. In His virgin birth, we see His holiness enter into creation. In his teaching, we find holy truth. In His miracles, we see His holy authority over creation. In His words, we find holy kindness and healing for broken souls. In His judgments, we find perfect, holy discernment. In His life, we find holy purity. In His trial, Pilot proclaimed His holy innocence (John 19:4), and yet He was condemned. In His crucifixion, we were extended His perfect, holy love. In His resurrection, we see His holy nature conquer death. Through our faith in Him we are lifted out of the temporal into His holiness.

Holy, Holy, Holy is the Lord. He alone is worthy of ceaseless praise from all who have breath. Lift your eyes to Him and know the heart of your King, the King of Glory.

Part 3 - God Is One
(Deut. 6:4-9; 11:13-21; Numbers 15:37-41)

Hear O Israel: The LORD our God, the LORD is One."

Duet. 6:4 (ESV)

Deuteronomy 6:4 is the first sentence of the Jewish prayer known as the Shema. Faithful Jews recognize the oneness of God as being foundational to their religion. They believe anything that compromises His oneness in any way should be soundly rejected. This is why they vehemently reject the Christian teaching of the triune nature of God. They understand that God is the ultimate, eternal singularity from which all things came into existence. A singularity, in its very essence, does not have multiple parts. I will attempt to address the Jewish concern at the end of this section.

In physics, a singularity is the point when a function takes on an infinite value. It is typically used as a reference to when matter becomes infinitely dense.

Black holes in Space are referred to as singularities.

As I'm writing this section, the Webb telescope is being launched into space as the successor to the Hubble. It is a state-of-the-art infrared telescope designed to probe the outer limits of the universe and gain more insight into our origins. It will also examine the massive black holes that exist at the center of galaxies to better understand the nature of these singularities. The concept of a singularity is well established in scientific theory.

The first singularity, according to theory, explains the source of matter from which the entire universe came into existence. The big bang theory begins with an infinitely dense speck of matter from which the universe exploded into existence.

However, as we discussed earlier, for a cause-and-effect universe to exist, some self-existent source is the necessary first cause. The idea that matter itself is self-existent defies all scientific methods of discovery and is a massive leap of faith. We have a choice. We can trust the reasoning of men or the self-revelation of the self-existing God. The only rational choice is that the cause-and-effect universe owes its existence to a self-existing infinite singularity described in scripture as the great I AM (Ex. 3:13,14; Jn. 8:56-59).

Christians can agree with scientific theory that the universe did actually "explode into existence" out of a singularity. But the ultimate singularity is not matter. It is the oneness of our self-existent God.

God's essential nature is indivisible, simply meaning that God cannot be divided into parts. This means that one aspect of God's eternal nature is never in conflict with another. Scripture declares that "God is one" (Deut. 6:4) and that in Him there is "No variation or shadow of changing" (James 1:17). There is a perfect harmonious unity within the nature of God.

There is a danger when we study His attributes of treating them as separate aspects of His nature.

An illustration may be helpful. Many perceive God's nature to work like a complicated machine with a set of dials, each of which represents one of His attributes. Then God, based on the circumstances, adjusts all the dials to guide His nature into a balanced response.

But the idea of God's oneness is that there is no need to balance His attributes. When God shows mercy He does not dial down justice and dial up love. Mercy reflects the fulness of His justice AND the fulness of His love. Likewise, in His wrath, He shows the fulness of His love AND justice.

A more accurate illustration of His oneness would be one dial that represents all of God's nature, everything that God is, and that dial is eternally set at 100%.

Of all of God's interactions with mankind, the one that may best illustrate His oneness is the cross. At the cross, His justice was fulfilled, His love was demonstrated, His power was unleashed, and His sovereign plan was accomplished. Even His eternal nature was revealed by one event that occurred in the course of time when Christ died for sins past, present and future, and He reconciled the universe to Himself (Romans 5:8-10).

God's nature is one. If we find ourselves trying to explain His actions by creating a balancing act between His attributes, we are tampering with His oneness. If you think that in His wrath, God's love is lessened in order to put His justice on display, or if you think that God's sovereignty is limited by man's freedom of choice, you are tampering with His nature.

If we lose sight of God's oneness, we will inevitably begin to create a "god" in our own image. Mankind's commitment to love, goodness, and justice will vacillate from one set of circumstances to another. God's does not. His nature is a Holy singularity.

This is an important principle to remember through life's pain and sorrow. In Psalm 88, the Psalmist feels overwhelmed and abandoned by God. God's wrath flows over him in waves of despair. But in the middle of His distress, he remembered God and cried out to Him (Ps. 88:13). It is in these darkest moments, when our soul has lost hope, that we must remember His oneness.

There is no possibility that God will ever withdraw His love from you or from all of mankind. On top of that, His oneness tells us He has the wisdom and the power to bring into your life what is eternally best for you. His infinite wisdom, power and love, along with all aspects of His essential nature, are fully at work as He cares for you and all of His creation.

When you know that God's nature is one, there is no basis for fear. Under no circumstance will His need for justice ever contort His nature into a harsh, vindictive deity. God does not balance one aspect of His nature against another.

Sound doctrine should never place one aspect of God's eternal nature in conflict with another. God is One.

Let's now return to the Jewish concern with the Christian doctrine of a triune God. Does this doctrine violate the oneness of God? As we will see in the section on God is Relational, the scripture teaches that a singular, unified relationship resides at the heart of God. The focus of the trinity is that God is the singular, self-existent source of a perfect, unified relationship. The relationship is holy. It was not created by God. It is self-existent within the nature of God. We find relationships within creation because God is relational. The persons of the Father, Son and Holy Spirit are the unified, singular fabric to which all relationships owe their existence. The doctrine of the trinity does not violate the oneness of God. It explains the reality of a perfect relational oneness at the heart of God and the promise to us who believe that we, too, will one day exist in that oneness (John 17:20,21).

We can rejoice in His oneness. It assures us that in everything God does, He can be trusted. We may not understand, but we can trust that His actions always reflect the oneness of His nature.

Part 4 – God Is Eternal
(Deut. 33:27; Ps. 90:2; 1 Tim. 1:17)

"... I am the Alpha and the Omega, the first and the last, the beginning and the end."

Revelation 22:13 (ESV)

The Greek and Hebrew words used for the concept of time can be challenging to translate. When you see the word eternal in the New Testament, it is most likely the Greek word aiónios. The literal translation of this word is an age or pertaining to an age[1] (note 1 below). The word does not focus on the duration of the age. It is concerned about some quality that characterizes the time period.

The duration of time is secondary at best.

We express a similar idea in English with sayings such as: "The age of jazz," "The information age," and "The age of enlightenment." There is some aspect of that loosely defined period of time that we are bringing to attention. It is the characteristic of the age, not its duration, that is germane to the conversation.

Let's consider a familiar scriptural example. John 3:16 (ESV) says, "For God so loved the world, that he gave his only Son, that whoever believes in him should not perish but have **eternal** life." Followers of Christ possess aionios life or age life. We live on the timeline of this world but possess a life that is not of this world. The point is not that we will live forever. It is much more significant than that. We possess a life from God that is timeless. It is boundless. Believers in this age live a life of unspecified duration, but they possess a timeless, boundless

---

1   aiónios – Strong's Greek 166 aiónios (an adjective, derived from 165 /aión ("an age, having a particular character and quality") – properly, "age-like" ("like-an-age"), i.e., an "age-characteristic" (the quality describing a particular age); (figuratively) the unique quality (reality) of God's life at work in the believer, i.e., as the Lord manifests His self-existent life (as it is in His sinless abode of heaven). "Eternal (166 /aiónios) life operates simultaneously outside of time, inside of time, and beyond time – i.e., what gives time its everlasting meaning for the believer through faith, yet is also time-independent. See 165 (aión). [166 (aiónios) does not focus on the future per se, but rather on the quality of the age (165 /aión) it relates to. Thus, believers live in "eternal (166 /aiónios) life" right now, experiencing this quality of God's life now as a present possession. (Note the Gk present tense of having eternal life in Jn 3:36, 5:24, 6:47; cf. Ro 6:23.)] (Bible Hub)

eternal life. We should never reduce the meaning of eternal life to living forever. It is the quality, not the timeframe, that is being proclaimed in Jn. 3:16.

Believers possess a life that has blown the doors off creation's boundaries. Eternal life is the essential nature of God. God's glory has entered His creation in us. The character of life that we see in God has been given to us. He is giving His Holy nature to us. This is eternal life. It is life flowing to us from the essence of God, who has no boundaries.

When eternal is used to describe the nature of God, it means infinitely more than living forever. It means He lives apart from time. His existence is not measured by the ticking of a clock. I suspect that when we think of God as living forever, it is actually a form of idolatry. We are allowing creation's concept of time to shape our understanding of God rather than focusing on His self-revelation in scripture.

To say that God is eternal is to say that He exists without limitation. He is unconstrained in every way. Finite creation cannot place any boundaries on Him.

When we begin to realize that His eternal life is in us who believe, our fears and doubts should begin to fade. Why? Because it is life without boundaries. All the promises He has made to us will be fulfilled in us because there is nothing that can limit His ability to do as He says. He is eternal. He has no limits. The apostle Paul put it this way: "All the promises of God are yes in Him, that is why we say AMEN to the glory of God." II Cor. 1:20 (ESV). Paul's confidence was founded on the essential nature of our limitless God, and so should ours.

I would also like to consider how God's eternal nature will be revealed to unbelievers. Matthew 24:46 (ESV) says, "And they (the lost) will go away into eternal punishment, but the righteous into eternal life.". Believers enter into aionios life and unbelievers into aionios judgment. We've already discussed what aionios life means for believers. Let's look at the flip side of that coin, the aionios punishment of the lost.

Just as eternal life is the experience of life as it exists apart from creation's timeline, so is eternal judgment. The lost will enter into an experience of God's judgment that is timeless and boundless. It is not measured by time. It is eternal judgment. This judgment, just like the life believers experience, will perfectly and completely reflect the oneness of God's eternal nature.

Unbelievers will experience the same God as believers. There is not a kind God for believers and a harsh God for unbelievers. God is one, and His actions toward both believers and unbelievers will flow from the oneness or singularity of His nature.

His actions toward believers and unbelievers are clearly not the same. But all His actions will fully embody every aspect of His nature. The more we know what God is really like, the more we can trust Him in His judgment of the lost. This is critical to understand as we read scripture. If we think that God shows love in His actions to believers and justice to unbelievers, we are tampering with His nature. Every action is always 100% love and 100% just. It is 100% of all that God is. He never balances one aspect of His nature against another.

God's nature is one.

Just as John 3:16 does not focus on the duration of eternal life but its qualities, the same is true about Matthew 24:46. The unbeliever will enter an age of unspecified duration in which they experience eternal judgment. It is a judgment without boundaries that will manifest the fullness of God's nature to them and expose them at the deepest level.

The parable of Lazarus and the rich man makes it clear that God's judgment will be a crushing pain for the lost (Luke 16:19-31). However, we should never have to explain God's judgment as some twisted distortion of His nature.

Judgment is not God settling the score with sinners. The beauty of His nature must guide our understanding of His judgment. I will speak at greater length about this in the "God is Love" chapter.

To summarize, when the word aionios is translated as eternal, it describes God's nature and His interactions with mankind. It is not tied to some human concept of the passage of time. The meaning is the exact opposite of that. The word draws attention to the character of an age (life or judgment), not its duration.

There is another Greek word that is a time word. That word is aidios (See note 2 below). It is translated as eternal or everlasting from the root meaning ever doing. It means always happening. Its use was common practice, at least in the non-religious literature of the first century, to express uninterrupted time or time of endless duration. It is only used twice in the New Testament as follows:

Rom. 1:20 (ESV) For his invisible attributes, namely, his **eternal** *power and divine nature, have been clearly perceived, ever since the creation of the world, [a] in the things that have been made. So they are without excuse.*

Jude 6 (ESV) And the angels who did not stay within their own position of authority, but left their proper dwelling, he has kept in **eternal** *chains under gloomy darkness until the judgment of the great day—*

Aidios[2] is used to describe a perpetual, unbroken period of time. If endless time was what Matthew was communicating regarding life and judgment, aidios would have been the proper choice of words. But the Holy Spirit chose aionios, which puts emphasis on the character of life and the judgment flowing from God onto mankind.

Can you see how aidios is used in the above two verses to emphasize perpetual unbroken time?

The first New Testament usage of aidios describes God's power as perpetually on display in creation (Rom. 1:20). It means as long as time and creation exist, God's power will be on display. Notice how, in this verse, the display of God's power is directly tied to the timeline in the phrase "ever since the creation of the world." With aidios, God is using time and creation to help man perceive His power. With aionios, God is pulling man outside of time to experience His eternal nature. Believers experience His eternal life and the lost experience His eternal judgement. All of mankind will enter into His presence and see Him as He is in His essential nature.

---

2   aidios – Strong's Greek 126 aidios (From aei; everduring (forward and backward, or forward only) – eternal, everlasting.).

The second New Testament usage of aidios describes the imprisonment of the fallen angels perpetually over time until judgment day (Jude 6). While the Romans verse describes everlasting as being directly tied to all of time, the Jude verse has a beginning and an end. The everlasting in this verse begins when the fallen angels are placed in chains, and it lasts perpetually, without interruption, until the "judgment of the great day."

Aidios is the word that describes perpetual, uninterrupted time, not aionios.

When we see the word eternal in the English Bible, it is usually translated from the Greek word aionios. If we read the passage thinking it is referring to something that continues perpetually for all of time we are missing the point. In so doing, we can also compromise the boundless, timeless nature of God.

God is eternal does not mean He lives forever. It means He lives apart from forever. What a glorious reality to ponder.

I pray that He would draw you deeper into the reality of His boundless, unlimited life. It is His gift to all believers. The more we discern about His eternal nature, the more we'll find His life growing in our personal experience. The more boundaries we place on Him, the more limited our experience of His life in us.

Jesus describes eternal life with these words: "I am the vine; you are the branches. Whoever abides in me and I in him, he it is that bears much fruit, for apart from me you can do nothing" (John 15:5 ESV) God's Son is the vine, rooted in eternity, from which boundless life flows into creation for all who believe.

Lord, open our eyes and illuminate our understanding as we focus our thoughts on you.

Part 5 – God Is Immutable
(Malachi 3:6; Ps 102:26,27)

There is unwavering peace today when an uncertain tomorrow is trusted to an unchanging God.

Ann Voskamp

Malachi 3:6 "For I the Lord do not change; therefore you, O children of Jacob, are not consumed."

1 Samuel 15:29 And also the Glory of Israel will not lie or have regret, for he is not a man, that he should have regret."

Hebrews 13:8 Jesus Christ is the same yesterday and today and forever.

James 1:17 Every good gift and every perfect gift is from above, coming down from the Father of lights, with whom there is no variation or shadow due to change.

The idea of someone who never changes sounds kind of mundane to me. Day after day, nothing changes; nothing is new, just the same old routine. It reminds me of Bill Murray living the same day over and over in the movie "Ground Hog Day." Is that what God is like?

Let's start with what immutable is not. It does not mean that every day with God is like the prior. That would be immutably boring. Every day with God is a new and unpredictable adventure. It does not mean that God cannot "change His mind" in temporal relationships with mankind. In fact, it does appear, on several occasions in scripture, that He not only can change His mind, but he can also regret a prior decision (Gen. 6:5-6 ESV "The Lord saw that the wickedness of man was great in the earth and that every intention of the thoughts of his heart was only evil continually. And the Lord regretted that he had made man on the earth, and it grieved him to his heart.") Also see Ex. 32:14; Jonah 3:10; 2 Sam. 24:16.

The Gen. 6:5,6 passage sounds like a major change in God. He went from saying His creation of mankind was very good (Gen. 1:31) to regretting that He had even made mankind on the earth (Gen. 6:5,6). What's going on here, and what does it teach us about God?

When you compare Gen. 6:5-6 to 1 Sam.15:29 (above), they appear to be in direct conflict. One verse says God will have no regrets, but the other says He regretted making man. Both verses use the same Hebrew word, "nacham," which, like many Hebrew words, carries a variety of meanings based on context.

Dr. Sandra Richter, author of "Epic of Eden," described Hebrew words as pigments on an artist's pallet. Just as an artist blends the pigments in a wide variety of ways to create a picture that is more than the sum of its parts, the Hebrew author blends words, each of which can carry a variety of meanings, into a story that can only be understood in its full context. Greek, on the other hand, analyzes and describes an idea. Hebrew is like a painting, and Greek is more like a photograph.

The Hebrew word nacham can mean (From Brown-Driver_Briggs on Bible Hub)

1. be sorry, moved to pity, have compassion for others, absolute
2. be sorry, rue, suffer grief, repent of one's own doings, absolute
3. comfort oneself, be comforted: Absolute
4. comfort oneself, ease oneself, by taking vengeance with

Consider the breadth of meaning in this one Hebrew word. It covers the range of motivation from sorrow for what others are experiencing to sorrow over one's own behavior to a desire for personal comfort and even vengeance. It can be directed toward oneself or others. It can produce both compassion and vengeance. And context informs how it should be understood.

I Samual 15:29 means that every decision God ever makes will be in perfect harmony with His character. Thus, He will never think He made a mistake and regret His actions. In other words, His nature is immutable; it will never change. He is flawless, pure, and holy. Any change in God's nature whatsoever would be a corruption of that beauty.

God will never change His mind because He has discovered something new that influences His actions. And yet, in His relationship with mankind, we do see God frequently changing His mind in response to their choices. But these are changes in God's relationship with mankind. They are not changes in His nature. So what picture of God is Moses (author of Genesis) creating for us in Gen. 6:6? Look at the previously discussed 4 meanings of nacham. Was God's "regret" for creating us motivated by His compassion for lost mankind, or did He think He made a mistake?

If we think this verse is teaching that God is in any way questioning Himself about the creation of mankind, we are distorting His nature. God was not having a moment of self-doubt. He was expressing compassion for the suffering that sin had brought onto mankind.

Immutability applies to His unchanging essential nature, not His relationship with a temporal creation.

God's character cannot be corrupted, nor can it be improved. It is immutable.

No amount of evil and dysfunction will ever cast its shadow across the character of God. God's response to evil is always a perfect and complete reflection of all of His eternal attributes in all of their fullness. Evil will never lessen or change the nature of His love, His justice or any other aspect of His eternal nature in His response. This is always true, whether His response is to patiently wait, to extend grace or to execute judgment.

This means that not only can His nature never be compromised, but neither can it be improved. So you can trust the unchanging perfection of His nature. Rest assured, from the eyes of eternity, you, along with all of mankind, are being guided by His perfect wisdom, discerning justice, and steadfast love. You can trust the goodness of His unchanging nature.

Reflect on His immutability and know that He can be trusted with your greatest and most private concerns.

Part 6 – God is Relational
(Gen. 1:26; Rom. 5:10, 8:15; John 17:21)

... but you have received the Spirit of adoption as sons, by whom we cry, "Abba! Father!"

Romans 8:15 (ESV)

I believe it would be impossible to overestimate the implications of the relational nature of God for the human race. Apart from this aspect of His nature, the deists would be right. God would simply be an impersonal source of ultimate power and authority. He would be the potter and we would be nothing more than clay to be used for His purposes and then discarded.

Surprisingly, the metaphor of the potter and the clay is used frequently in scripture (Is. 46:8; Romans 9:20,21; Jer. 18:4). We are clay in His hands being shaped for His purpose. But as we will see in this section, His purpose is a perfect, eternal relationship. His relational nature makes the notion that He could use us and then discard us an absurdity.

The Bible is fundamentally a story about God's relationship with His creation. The story begins in Genesis 1. We discussed Genesis 1:1 in the chapter on God's self-existence. With the words "In the beginning God..." we met the self-existent One from whom all of creation originated. He was introduced as the source or fountainhead of all creation.

In Genesis 1:26 (ESV), we discover something new about God with the words, "Let **us** make man in **our image**, after **our likeness**.". God is describing His nature or likeness using plural language. And yet, we just explained in a previous section that God is One. Is His nature one, or is it plural? This may sound like a conflict, but it is not difficult to explain.

God's essential nature is one, and all His responses to creation reflect that oneness. His actions are always a perfect and complete expression of all of His attributes. One attribute is never compromised, so another attribute can take priority over it. This idea of God's oneness does not contradict what we are discovering in Genesis 1:26. But it does inform it.

What Genesis 1:26 tells us is that relationship is at the core of God's image or His likeness. Within God's nature, there exists a unified plurality or an us-ness

- *"Let us make man in our image."* God's oneness tells us what that us-ness is like. It is a relationship of perfect and infinite unity.

The apostle John further develops the relational nature of God throughout his gospel. It begins with these words:

John 1:1-3 (ESV) – *In the beginning **was the Word**, and the **Word was with God**, and the **Word was God**. He was in the beginning with God. **All things were made through him**, and without him was not any thing made that was made.*

These verses point back to Genesis 1, which starts with the words "In the beginning God." We are reminded that God is self-existing outside of time and the material universe. In the same way, **Jesus** (The Word that became flesh – John 1:14) **is self-existing** outside of creation. He is also proclaimed to have **created all things**. He was/is **with God** in a perfect, self-existing relationship. And **He was/is God,** meaning Jesus is everything that God is. This is a declaration of the perfect relational oneness within the nature of God. John blasts open the door into the mystery of the relational nature of God. He had witnessed it firsthand as Jesus's disciple. He was the disciple who experienced Jesus' love like none other. He even referred to himself as the disciple Jesus loved (John 21:7). It is from that intimate experience that he draws us into the relational nature, or the us-ness, of God like no other Biblical author.

At the core of His being, God is relational.

This is wonderful news. God will always relate to us according to the principles of relational perfection as He draws us into unity with Himself. Jesus announced this same relational oneness in John 10:30 when He said, "I and the Father are one." This had to be a stunning statement to the ears of His audience. He was claiming that His relational unity with His Father was an aspect of God's oneness. To the Jewish mind, the idea of relational oneness within the nature of God must have been an earth-shattering revelation. They could not reconcile the idea of multiple "persons" within the nature of God, and the scripture that teaches God is one (Deut. 6:4). And for 2000 years, it has remained a stumbling block between them and their messiah.

The scripture has made it clear that the essence of God's nature is relational. Relationships are not just something God does, nor are they something that He created. His very essence is relational. To know Him is to enter into that relationship. A believer is saved into this triune relationship. That's the point Paul is making in 2 Cor. 5:20 when he says, "We implore you on behalf of Christ, be reconciled to God." It is an invitation to step into the very nature of God and be transformed in this new relationship of perfect unity.

My favorite New Testament example of this is found in Jesus' words as He prayed with His disciples in John 17:21 (ESV) *"that they may all be one, just as you, Father, are in me, and I in you, that they also may be in us, so that the world may believe that you have sent me."* The ultimate goal of salvation is not to go to heaven. Heaven is our destination, but the perfect unity of this relationship is our destiny.

Jesus's prayer expresses the heartbeat of the gospel. The gospel is an invitation to be reconciled into this relationship with God and others. The singular relationship at the heart of God is the meaning of eternal life. Accepting Jesus to avoid Hell and its consequences is not the focus of the gospel message. The gospel message is that in Christ, God has reconciled the world to Himself and He is inviting us into that reconciliation (2 Cor. 5:19,20). He is inviting us into Himself, into His family. He becomes our Abba, our Daddy, and in Him, we begin a relational transformation from death to life.

In Col 1:15-23, Paul describes the cosmic scope of this gospel of reconciliation. In verse 20, he says:

"and through him to reconcile to himself all things, whether on earth or in heaven, making peace by the blood of his cross."

Notice the relational focus of the gospel in this verse. God's plan is to reconcile all things in all of creation into a relationship with himself. The verb reconcile is in the aorist tense, which means that God has already, at a point in time, accomplished that plan. At the cross, every sinner, even the most vile, was reconciled to God. Note that this is not simply the potential of reconciliation. At the cross, God reconciled every aspect of creation to Himself. It was finished.

The gospel proclaims that at the cross, God has reconciled mankind to Himself, and it then invites the individual sinner to receive that reconciliation and enter into His relational life.

The passage in Colossians describes the nature of this reconciliation and how it was accomplished. It is a reconciliation of peace (relational restoration) for all creation, accomplished by the blood of the cross.

Some teach that the reconciliation in Colossians 1:20 is not necessarily relational but simply means all mankind will be reconciled either to God's eternal plan of salvation or His eternal plan of condemnation[3] (see Note below). They teach that it is a relational reconciliation for believers, but for the lost, it is a forced submission. And yet the passage describes it as a relational reconciliation bringing peace by the blood of the cross. It's hard to imagine how a plan that condemns people to everlasting torment can be described as a reconciliation of peace accomplished by the blood of the cross. Why would the cross be needed to give people what they deserve?

Paul provides us with more insight into this gospel of reconciliation in Romans 5:10,11:

"For if while we were enemies we were reconciled to God by the death of his Son, much more, now that we are reconciled, shall we be saved by his life. More than that, we also rejoice in God through our Lord Jesus Christ, through whom we have now received reconciliation."

God's relationship with His creation was damaged by sin. In Christ, God has brought His perfect triune relationship into our mess and mankind responded by trying to destroy that relationship at the cross. If the unity within the trinity

---

3   Study notes from "The MacArthur Study Bible," copyright 1997
Man is reconciled to God when God restores man to a right relationship with Him through Jesus Christ. An intensified form for "reconcile" is used in this verse to refer to the total and complete reconciliation of believers and ultimately "all things" in the created universe (cf. Rom. 8:21; 2 Pet. 3:10-13; Rev. 21:1). This text does not teach that; as a result, all will believe; rather it teaches that all will ultimately submit (cf. Phil. 2:9-11)

could be demonstrated as flawed in any way, it's game over, and Satan wins. But God's nature was tested in every way on the stage of His creation, and in Christ, there is no hint of corruption. Death could not hold Him. And so a broken humanity was reconciled to God.

God's nature was on trial with the incarnation of Christ. Satan's argument has always been that God is not who He claims to be. I suspect Satan's taunt sounded something like this: "God if you think you are so perfect sitting there on your throne, try entering into your own creation, which is a mess, by the way, and show us how perfect you really are." And God responded.

In His life, Christ flawlessly put on display the nature of God in all His actions. And in His death, He demonstrated the flawless nature of His relational love in supreme sacrifice. In the life and death of Christ, God displayed His Holy nature in the form of flesh for mankind to witness. At the cross, the trial on God's nature was finished. If there was any flaw found in Him, Christ would have remained in the grave. But we know the story. The claims God makes about Himself in scripture were proven true in every way in Christ. And the result is a living Savior and a reconciled humanity.

God's nature has been tried on the stage of history and proven to be trustworthy. In a human trial, we are judged based on our behavior, but in Christ, God's nature, not just His behavior, was on trial. Even the slightest unseen blemish would result in a guilty verdict. If this were our trial, it would be certain guilt for the entire human race. But no guile was found in Him, and the verdict was "NOT GUILTY." The grave had to release its hold on Him. The beauty of God's nature revealed in scripture has been tested in creation and proven to be trustworthy. We can be confident that He is the very essence of perfect goodness and beauty.

Whenever we feel the need to tamper with God's nature to align it with our system of beliefs we are putting God's nature back on trial. When we find ourselves in this situation, it is our theology that should be put on trial and not God's nature.

A few examples of how we do this might be helpful. A tell-tell sign that we might be putting God's nature on trial is the use of the word but. "But" implies there is some exception about to be announced that places a limit on His nature.

Example 1 – "God is sovereign, **but** man also has free will." Can human choice ever, in any way, limit God's sovereignty? If the answer is yes, He is not sovereign over His creation, and His claim to be sovereign cannot be trusted.

The corrected statement is, "God is sovereign over all, including man's free will."

Example 2 – "God is love, **but** He has to deal with unrepentant sinners." Does my sin weaken God's love? If the answer is yes, then His love is conditional and cannot be trusted. The corrected statement is, "God is love, and perfect love will always guide His response to our sin."

Example 3 – "God is love, **but** He is also Just." In the first two examples, we use human behavior to cast a shadow of doubt across the nature of God. In this example, we suggest there is some internal conflict within the nature of God Himself. Does God set aside some aspect of His love in order to bring judgment on the unrepentant? If God's love is conditional, it is no longer an aspect of His eternal nature. This line of reasoning puts the nature of His love back on trial and pronounces Him guilty. The corrected statement is, "God is love, and He is Just." Everything He does is perfectly just and is a perfect application of His love. His oneness demands that His every thought and every action is always 100% just and 100% love.

If any of these examples were true, God could not be who He claims to be, and our hope of a perfect eternal relationship is lost. We are completely dependent on the perfection of God's eternal nature. If it is flawed in any way, Christ cannot be trusted. It is Satan who whispers the lying question in our ears; "Is God really that good?" He is the father of lies, and he loves the word, BUT.

However, in Christ, there are no "buts". Our relationship with Him is built on the perfection of His nature. There is no flaw, no shifting this way and that, in His nature. When you are tempted to think otherwise, it is Satan whispering the word "but" in your ear. God's nature was tested and proven true. There are no buts.

God is relational, and our relationship with Him is based on our absolute trust in His perfect, unchanging nature. Seeing His nature clearly, with no human distortions, is how our character is shaped. We become like Him by looking at Him. There are no lists of do's and don'ts, and there are no formulas that will ever produce spiritual growth. It is only as we center ourselves in a relationship with Him and peel back the layers of His infinite beauty that our worship is renewed and our nature continues to be transformed into His likeness.

Transformation happens as His nature becomes the filter or lens through which we see the world around us and the scriptural revelation God has given us.

Jesus described the centrality of this relationship in John 15:7-9:

"If you abide in me, and my words abide in you, ask whatever you wish, and it will be done for you. By this my Father is glorified, that you bear much fruit and so prove to be my disciples. As the Father has loved me, so have I loved you. Abide in my love."

Now, let's redirect our attention back to the cross.

There are those who hold to the idea that all the cross actually accomplished was to make salvation theoretically possible. They suggest the cross itself demonstrates God's love for mankind, but its real power is not unleashed until people choose to believe. Is the power of the cross found in a man's choice to believe? Or is the power of the cross inherent in itself? We need to make sure we have this right.

In John 1:9 (ESV), John the Baptist saw Jesus approaching and proclaimed: *Behold, the Lamb of God, who takes away the sin of the world!"*. When He saw Jesus, He understood an important truth. At the cross, Christ was the propitiation for all sin. He took away the sin of the world, and He reconciled the world to Himself.

I John 2:2 (ESV) – *"He is **the propitiation** for our sins, and not for ours only but also **for the sins of the whole world**."*

2 Cor. 5:19 (ESV) – *that is, **in Christ God was reconciling the world to himself**, not counting their trespasses against them, and entrusting to us the message of reconciliation.*

Consider again Paul's words in Ro. 5:10: *"while we were enemies we were reconciled to God."*. At the cross, all of mankind, while they were still enemies, were reconciled to God. It doesn't say all of mankind was justified. It doesn't say they were saved. Justification requires faith. Salvation is personally receiving and experiencing the reconciliation accomplished at the cross. But Christ's death did accomplish something for all mankind. In Christ, God reconciled "all things in heaven and earth" (Col. 1:20) to himself. He reconciled His enemies. Mankind was reconciled to God.

The gospel proclaims that Christ has broken sin's power over the human race and reconciled mankind to Himself. It is an invitation to receive that reconciliation and enter into life. Christ's death at the cross unilaterally reconciled creation back to God. It's like the 12-step program for the human race. God made amends for all the relational violations that have ever happened. From the trivial to the egregious, the amends have been made at the cross and reconciliation accomplished. The gospel message is this: God has made amends on our behalf, *"We implore you on behalf of Christ, be reconciled to God."*

The message of the gospel is an invitation to receive that reconciliation and begin living in a new kind of relationship with God and others. Jesus explained it to His disciples in this way: *"A new commandment I give to you, that you love one another: just as I have loved you, you also are to love one another." (John 13:34).* Loving others was not a new commandment. What was new was entering into God's triune relationship and discovering the infinite beauty of His perfect love. The second half of the Rom. 5:10,11 passage makes it clear that something new happens to us when we receive the reconciliation. It says, *"much more, now that we are reconciled, shall we be saved by his life. More than that, we also rejoice in God through our Lord Jesus Christ, through whom we have now received reconciliation."* The gospel is an invitation to receive the relational reconciliation that is already yours in Christ and begin to experience a new kind of life: perfect, eternal, relational life.

The scripture has just given us a glimpse into God's plan to bring everything back into unity with His relational nature. May I encourage you not to try to stuff this back into a theological box that makes you comfortable? Ask God to grant you a heart that desires and a mind that is ready to explore the wonders of His unsearchable nature. It is only there that we discover genuine Christian life.

Anything else is simply lifeless theology and a Christian self-improvement program. We must never settle for that.

In our next chapter we will look at how this relational unity operates and see why it must result in the reconciliation of all things that Paul was describing in Col. 1:20.

Part 7 – God Is Love
(I John 4:16; I Cor. 13; Matt. 22:36-40)

"Though our feelings come and go, God's love for us does not."

C. S. Lewis

It's hard to have a meaningful conversation about love. The word has been overused to the point that it has lost a lot of its relevance. I love ice cream. I love my dog. I love flowers. I love my child. I love my spouse. I love my work. I love God. I love golf. And then there's an unending stream of songs about love: 'Love Makes The World Go Round,' 'Love You Like A Love Song,' 'What's Love Got To Do With It,' 'Love Shack' and 'Crazy Little Thing Called Love.' The English word love is so broad that it has virtually lost any clear meaning. It's not surprising when the Bible says, "God is love" (1 John 4:16), we are left with a fairly muddled concept of what God is like.

Based on the English word love, it's almost inevitable that we will think of God as having an emotional, feelings-based kind of love. We project our concept of human love onto Him, thinking of Him as having a really good, even perfect, kind of human love. It is seeing God through the lens of ourselves and forming a distorted view of God. It's not possible to know God when we think in this manner. We should not look at ourselves to find out who God is. We should look at God to discover who we are. Fortunately, the Bible enables us to do just that.

The New Testament has a number of Greek words that can be translated into the English word love. One of those words describes the perfect love that is found in God. The Greek word is agape which I will either refer to as perfect love or as agape. When you hear agape, you should immediately think, "This is not talking about human love." It's not the best of human love. It is in a category by itself. It is separate from creation. It is a perfect, holy love.

Clarity about the meaning of agape is essential to properly understand scripture. It is so important that Jesus told His disciples that all of scripture hangs on or flows out of this perfect love (Matt 22:36-40). Paul prayed for followers of Christ not just to understand but to experience this agape love. It is through our relationship with God's agape that we grow in the goodness of God (Eph. 3:18,19). Our relational experience of God's agape is the essence of the Christian faith. If we get love right we'll get what is most important to God right.

God does not choose to love. He is love. Always, perfectly, 100%: God is love. God does choose how that love will be expressed. But there is no action that God will ever take that is not motivated by the fullness of His perfect love. It can never be said, about anything God ever does, that He is not acting in perfect agape love. There are those who believe that God's love is somehow diminished because He is also Just. Their reasoning goes like this: When God judges a sinner, His justice must take precedence over His love. They say, "Yes, God is love, but He is also Just". This perspective puts God's justice in conflict with His love. For justice to be served, love must decrease. This is a dangerous projection of human reason onto the nature of God. Both the fullness of His perfect agape love and the perfection of His justice motivate His every decision. It's not that His love is on display when He forgives, and His justice is on display when He judges. Remember that God is one!

If we look at the meaning of the Greek word agape, we are left wanting more. Agape focuses on a preference. In the New Testament, agape describes God's relational preferences. Agape is the way He loves and the way He desires us to love.

We are fortunate that the apostle Paul gave special attention to the meaning of agape in I Corinthians 13. If you study this passage carefully, there should be no doubt about what God's agape love is really like. It has been revealed to us. We just have to believe it. And that may require more faith than you realize.

We will focus on I Corinthians 13:4-8 (ESV):

"Love is patient and kind; love does not envy or boast; it is not arrogant or rude. It does not insist on its own way; it is not irritable or resentful; it does not rejoice at wrongdoing, but rejoices with the truth. Love bears all things, believes all things, hopes all things, endures all things. Love never ends..."

These verses describe 16 characteristics of God's perfect agape love. They are typically used as a personal application to develop in us a greater love for others. And, of course, that's something we should do. But additionally, because we know God is agape (I Jn 4:19), these verses also describe to us what God's perfect

50

agape love looks like in our fallen world. It shows us the manner in which God responds to everything in this world, including every detail of our individual lives. We can be certain He will always be motivated by and reflect all of these characteristics of love in everything He does.

All 16 characteristics are verbs in the Present Tense and the indicative mood. The Indicative mood is a statement of fact. Present tense means it occurs now, in the present moment. It is a fact that in every moment, love always responds in this way. In other words, there is no possibility that any of these characteristics of perfect love will be absent in any decision or action that God makes. Let's briefly consider each of the 16 aspects of God's love.

Love is Patient (makrothumeó) –

Meaning slow to anger with non-retaliatory anger (Bible Hub).

God's anger is an element of His agape love. And when agape does become angry, it is never out of revenge. Yes, perfect love does get angry, but it is still love. God's love does not turn into anger. His anger is not the opposite of love; it is an expression of His love. His anger has a love-based motivation. It is not vindictive, seeking to set the record straight or balance the scale of justice. That's the way man's anger behaves. James 1:20 (NIV) says, "the anger of man does not produce the righteousness God desires." The obvious conclusion is this: "The anger of God does produce the righteousness He desires." God's anger is motivated by His love. His anger is at work to produce goodness in the heart of an unrepentant sinner.

Let's consider an example. Johnathan Edwards portrays God in his book "Sinners in the Hands of an Angry God" as an offended, angry deity holding sinners over the fires of hell, ready to destroy them, just waiting for them to die to deliver their final judgment. The following is a famous quote from his book:

"The God that holds you over the pit of hell, much as one holds a spider or some loathsome insect over the fire, abhors you and is dreadfully provoked; his wrath towards you burns like fire; he looks upon you as worthy of nothing else, but to be cast into the fire ... you are ten thousand times so abominable in his eyes, as the most hateful and venomous serpent is in ours."

God does not abhor sinners. He abhors sin but loves sinners. His love for them is infinite and will never diminish. If you doubt this is true, keep reading. Because of His love, He died to take away the sins of the world (Jn 1:29). While we were yet sinners, Christ died for us and reconciled us to Himself (Rom 5:8-10). Edward's view of God is distorted. He's looking at God through His theology of judgment rather than looking at judgment through His relationship with God.

He then goes on to preach that you can escape this angry God by trusting in Him, at which point He will embrace you with His infinite love. Edwards sees God as either choosing love or choosing wrath. This is a false comparison. Love is an eternal attribute of God. His wrath is a temporal choice He makes when He interacts with sin. God's love is patient, meaning slow to anger. By meditating on this truth we discern that His anger is an expression of His love and not a conflicting attribute. His love can become angry, but that anger is still His love in action. I realize that it is much easier for us to see how God's forgiveness is an expression of His love. But the same is true for His wrath.

Edward's theological conclusions about God have seriously compromised His eternal nature. He has created a false image of God, which is idolatry. God is not bipolar. He's not an angry God who finds us disgusting but, at the same time, a Kind God who is willing to give us a chance. God is love: perfect, undiminished, fully engaged, eternal love.

As we continue through these 16 characteristics of God's love, my prayer is that we might grow together in our understanding of the glory of His infinite love and that we might feel a fire burning in our hearts, like the disciples on the road to Emmaus (Luke 24:13-25) experienced, as Jesus "explained the scriptures concerning Himself to them." May Jesus draw us deeper into worship and adoration of Him.

Love is Kind (chrésteuomai)

Meaning full of service to others (Bible Hub).

God's perfect love means His eyes are on us, not Himself. He knows the greatest need of every individual He created, and the motive of His love is to serve that need. There are times when God's goodness in our lives is clearly visible, like a newborn child or a restored relationship. But there are also times when God seems distant and uninterested in us and our prayers. We cry out, why doesn't God respond? Know this: His eye is on you, and He is actively serving your greatest need. You don't yet see this need, nor do you understand what is happening. But God is kind, which means that He is "full of service" toward you. Trust Him; like the parent taking candy out of a toddler's hand, God is actively serving you. It may feel like He is passive, but love is never passive.

Don't confuse this idea with a parent who enables dysfunction in their children. God is not serving what you think you need. His love is aggressively pursuing what He knows you need. He always has your back, even when it feels like He has abandoned you.

Remember Jesus's words on the cross: "My God, My God, Why have you forsaken me?". At that very moment, on the cross, when Jesus was experiencing your fears of abandonment, God was serving your greatest need. Jesus took your sin and lostness while God reconciled you to Himself. He is always "full of service" toward you.

We are invited to bring this kindness into the world as His disciples. May God allow us to see deeper into the needs of those around us and guide us in finding ways to serve those needs.

Love does not Envy (zéloó)

Meaning to earnestly desire (Bible Hub).

This word is often used in a positive sense. Paul said in I Cor. 12:31 to "earnestly desire the greater gifts." In II Cor. 11:2, he said, "I'm jealous for you with a godly jealousy. I promised you to one husband, to Christ, so that I might present you as a pure virgin to him." However, in the I Cor. 13 passage it is used in a negative perspective. Love is NOT an ungodly jealousy or envy.

Love would never earnestly desire to take something from someone that would in any way limit what is best for them. God would never remove something good from you because He wants it for Himself. For example, the love of your life has taken ill and is lying on their death bed. The thought occurs to you that you have done some bad things in your life, and now God is settling the score. Or maybe the sappy idea comes to your mind that God wants another angel in heaven.

God's love would never demand something from you to gratify Himself. God is certainly at work in every life crisis, but it is never motivated by some personal desire He is trying to satisfy, such as revenge or adding another buddy in heaven. How do I know this? God's jealousy for you is pure. His earnest desire is for you, not from you.

Cast far from your thoughts any idea that suggests God earnestly desires to settle the score with you. No matter how messed up or broken you are, God is always and forever for you because God does not envy you.

Love does not Boast (perpereuomai)

Meaning to act as a braggart, i.e., a "show off" who needs too much attention (used only in 1 Cor 13:4) (Bible Hub).

If anyone has the right to brag, it would be God. Yet God quietly revealed himself to the prophets, and now, through their efforts and His Spirit's work in us, the Scripture helps us see the truth about Him. He would certainly have the right to constantly remind us of His greatness, but instead, He chooses to quietly show himself to those who earnestly seek Him. The incarnation of Christ was God's greatest act of self-revelation. Yet He chose to quietly enter creation by slipping into a stable with smelly animals. He chose to submit himself to human parents. He graciously taught about the glory of the Father while living in humility. He became a servant and washed His disciples' feet. His love is so other focused there is no hint of being an attention seeker. Compare Him to the cult leaders of our day and the difference is striking.

One day, when we stand before Him, His focus will not be on reminding us how great He is. His focus will be on you, not himself. He will not make sure you know how badly you have violated His greatness. His perfect love will be on display at the judgment, and for those who believe, our hearts will melt in adoration.

Love is not Arrogant (phusioó)

Meaning swelled up, like an egotistical person spuing out arrogant ("puffed-up") thoughts (Bible Hub).

This word describes the inward heart attitude that produces boasting. Arrogant people consider themselves to be so far above everyone else that they look down on others. I unfortunately made the mistake one time of hiring an arrogant young man. He would refer to himself as "a racehorse working among plow horses." Needless to say, he wasn't much of a team player.

God's love is not like this. He is infinitely more than the best of humanity, and yet there is not a hint of arrogance in Him. He will not be condescending and remind us of His awesome greatness. Yet, in His presence, we will be undone by His glory. For us who believe, all of our rationalizations for sin will melt away, and we will be eternally cleansed, perfectly reflecting His goodness. Arrogance tries to make others feel small. God's love always draws us higher.

Love is not Rude (aschémoneó)

Meaning to act unseemly (literally, "improperly"); (figuratively) to lack proper form and hence be thought of as unseemly (indecent, unbecoming) (Bible Hub).

Love is sensitive to how its behavior will be perceived by other people. It would never callously do something to intentionally offend others. Rudeness closes the heart.

In contrast, perfect love is always gracious and edifying, desiring what is best for another person. God's love may offend and it may make us uncomfortable. It may even bring us great pain, but it is motivated by His goodness and it is seeking a constructive outcome. This is always true of God's behavior, no matter how harsh that behavior may seem from a human perspective. Even something as violent as the great flood is motivated by everything that God is, including His love for each person who perished.

When we find things like the flood in scripture that cause us to doubt the nature of God's love, we need His help to understand His perspective and motivation. So, how can I find God's help in doing this? How do I understand the flood in the light of His nature? We start with a change in our perspective.

Unfortunately, we tend to look at things from our human perspective and ask: "How do I understand God in light of the flood?". It is a human tendency to look at events in this world, even those found in scripture, and draw conclusions about God. We see people killed in an earthquake or suffering from disease, and we ask, "How can a God who claims to be all-powerful and whose love is perfect allow this?". It is the normal flow of human logic to start with the familiar (the events of this world) and draw conclusions about the unfamiliar (the nature of God). That's how our minds tend to function.

But this kind of human logic can lead us to believe false narratives about God. In fact, we can start to see God as frustrated with our lack of moral progress and becoming quite harsh in His response. We say things like God was patient for 120 years before the flood, and He repeatedly warned them. They had their chance to repent and finally got what they deserved. In this narrative we are trying to understand God's nature by looking at the events of the flood.

We need to reverse the flow of logic and start with God and then draw conclusions about the events we see in this world. What might change if we first look at God's nature and then ask, "What does this tell me about the flood?"

Let's look at the flood through the lens of the first 6 aspects of God's love we just discussed.

1. God's love is patient. It includes an element of anger, but it is unlike the anger of man. God's anger has the purpose of producing righteousness.
2. God's love is kind. It is full of service to others. He knows and seeks to satisfy your deepest needs.
3. God's love does not envy. He is forever for you, never demanding from you.
4. God's love does not boast. He does not focus on Himself at all. He doesn't try to impose His greatness on you. His focus is on you.
5. God's love is not arrogant. He would never compare Himself to you in order to put you in your place. His love seeks to lift you up.
6. God's love is not rude. He would never do anything that would be inappropriate.

If you consider just these six of the sixteen aspects of God's love to help you understand the great flood, your perspective will begin to change. Every person impacted by the flood was experiencing these 6 aspects of God's love plus the ten we have yet to discuss. The flood was an act of God's judgment that perfectly reflects 100% of His love, His justice, His holiness, His Oneness etc.

100% of all that He is was revealed to those who perished in the flood. We can speculate about a lot of things, but this is not speculation. We may not understand how the judgment is an act of God's love, but by faith, we believe it to be true. It must be because God is love. And by faith alone, as we experience His love, we are learning to love like Him.

The theme of God's judgment occurs repeatedly throughout scripture and we are often left with the impression that God is kind and patient until He reaches the end of His fuse and then He blows up. This is a human understanding of love and does not reflect God's nature at all. When we read sections of scripture that sound like God finally loses it and goes ballistic, we must never minimize in any way the love of God at work in the midst of judgment. The waters of the Red Sea that destroyed the Pharaoh and his army in judgment were motivated by God's love. The fiery images of the final judgment are motivated by love just as much as the forgiveness of a repentant sinner.

I understand that what I'm saying is beyond our comprehension. But that is exactly the point I am making. God is love. He does not choose to love, depending on the circumstances. Human love may falter, but not God's. As we continue in I Corinthians 13, we are learning what perfect love actually looks like, and in so doing, we are seeing the heart of God.

So, let's continue.

Love Does not Insist on its Own Way (zéteó)

Meaning properly, to seek by inquiring; to investigate to reach a binding (terminal) resolution; to search, "getting to the bottom of a matter." (Bible Hub).

This is an important aspect of God's love that helps us understand the world in which we live. People often ask the question, how could a loving God allow so much evil in the world? This may seem a bit counterintuitive, but it is exactly because God is love that he allows evil to continue. Love does not insist on its own way. God's love knows what is best for each individual, but it does not force compliance. This is an aspect of God's love that Satan has exploited from the beginning. In the process of God's plan to reconcile the universe to himself (Col 1), he will never violate this or any aspect of love. This characteristic of God's perfect love is the principle on which our understanding of man's freedom of choice is based. Without it, human choice would not be possible.

It also helps us understand God's patience. Love is patient or slow to anger because it doesn't insist on its own way. This is one of the things that makes God's glory so unsearchable. The beauty of our God, who does not insist on getting His own way, is that all things will ultimately be conformed to His will. What? That sounds like double-speak. Listen carefully; the unsearchable riches of His glory will draw, not force, all things into reconciliation with Him. Such is the power of the cross (Col. 1:20). How is this possible? His goodness is an eternal reality. Evil is not. C S Lewis believed that evil is a corruption of goodness. Evil could not even exist if goodness did not first exist. Goodness is transcendent and eternal. Evil is temporal and passing. God does not have to insist on His own way because evil and corruption are not eternal; they hold no real power, nor can they endure. They exist only because God's love does not insist on its own way.

Consider how God's love for you will never demand that you do things His way. In His love, He invites you to participate in eternity but allows you to continue living in the temporal insanity of this world. In what ways are you refusing God's invitation to grow in His goodness?

Love is not Irritable (paroxunó)

Meaning properly, cut close alongside, i.e., to incite "ja") someone and stimulate their feelings (emotions); "become emotionally provoked (upset, *roused to anger*" (*A-S*), as *personally* "getting to someone"; (figuratively)"*to provoke feelings, spurring* someone to action" (Souter) (Bible Hub)

This Greek word is a feelings-based, reactionary anger. It describes the anger of men, which has no place in perfect love. When we discussed "Love is Slow to Anger," we observed that God's anger is always patient and motivated by His love. But man's anger cannot coexist with perfect love. When we think of God as having an emotional, feelings-based type of anger, we are distorting His character. We saw how Johnathan Edwards did this in his book "Sinners in the Hands of an Angry God." He described God as "dreadfully provoked". But this verse says love is not irritable, meaning "to *provoke feelings, spurring* someone to action." Edwards literally ascribed to God a flawed, feelings-based human anger. God's agape has no element of human anger.

If you ever think that your sin is so great or so entrenched that God has given up on you, you are creating a God in your own image. Human anger gives up and moves on. Don't ever think of God in this way. As we progress through the 16 characteristics of agape love, we will see the eternal, unchanging commitment of God's love for mankind.

Love is not Resentful, or more literally, keeps no account of wrongs (logizomai, kakos)

Meaning **3049** *logízomai* (the root of the English terms *"logic, logical"*) – properly, *compute*, "take into account"; *reckon* (come to a"bottom-lin"), i.e. *reason* to a *logical conclusion* (decision). **2556** *kakós* (an adjective, and the root of 2549 / *kakía*, "inner malic") – properly, inwardly *foul, rotten* (*poisoned*); (figuratively) inner *malice* flowing out of a *morally-rotten* character ("the rot is already in the wood").

The word resentful is the translation of two Greek words. The first is to keep an account and the second is inner malice flowing out of a morally-rotten character. God's agape love does not keep a record of the evil deeds committed against it. This is wonderful news for the human race. God is not maintaining a scorecard that will one day be rubbed in your face. No matter how long the list of our sins has become, it is our list, not God's. To think that the evil in your heart has grown larger than God's love for you is idolatry. This aspect of God's love is demonstrated in the parable of the father's love for the prodigal son (Luke 15:11-32). The father did not keep a record of his son's wrongs. He did not insist on his own way. He waited until his son turned to him, and then his love embraced him.

God's love never diminishes, no matter how broken and dysfunctional we've become. We cannot sin our way out of God's love. At any time, we can turn to Him, and His love will bring into our lives what we need, not what we want and not what we deserve. If we chose to remain in our sin His love is still for us as sin takes its toll on our souls.

Love does not rejoice at wrongdoing (adikía)

Meaning properly, the *opposite* of *justice*; unrighteousness, as a *violation* of God's *standards* (*justice*) which brings *divine disapproval*; a count (violation) of *God's justice*, i.e., what is contrary to His *righteous judgments* (what He approves) (Bible Hub)

The placement of this characteristic of love in the list of 16 is important. We just looked at the idea that God's love does not keep a record of wrongs. But He does see evil, and it grieves His heart. His reaction when He sees sin is to the damage inflicted on mankind whom He loves. His love deeply disapproves of every violation of His justice. God's love will never overlook our sin, but love's response to sin is unrelentingly for our good.

We should not think that God's love gives us a license to sin. The wages of sin is death (Romans 6:23). With sin comes dysfunction and broken lives. Sin traps us in a prison of hopelessness. God's love for us is not diminished, but our ability to experience that love is severely damaged by our own sins and the sins of others. Perfect love grieves as it watches people sink deeper into sin's prison.

Love Rejoices (sugchairó) with the Truth (alétheia)

Meaning of Rejoices-- sharing God's grace with another person so that both rejoice together (mutually participate in God's favor and grace). (Bible Hub) Meaning of Truth-- truth, but not merely truth as spoken; truth of idea, reality, sincerity, truth in the moral sphere, divine truth revealed to man, straightforwardness. (Bible Hub)

The idea conveyed in these two words is that agape celebrates honesty in the moral sphere. Once we understand that God does not keep a record of wrong, but He does grieve to see how our sin damages those He loves, including us, we begin to realize that we have the freedom to confess our sins. Love rejoices when we openly share with God and others that we have, in some manner, been living in conflict with moral truth. The rejoicing is grace-centric because we have confessed our sins so that we may be healed.

Notice the progression of the last three characteristics. God's love never keeps a record of wrong. Why? So that we can be certain His desire is not to harm us but to heal us. We know that what He hates is not us but the damage our sin causes. Agape love sets us free to truthfully take our sin to Him and the people we have harmed with no excuses and no rationalization. When we transparently expose our moral failures to God, His presence is a no-condemnation zone.

God's love frees us to continually take our brokenness to Him because He rejoices when we are willing to expose the darkest secrets of our inner person.

Love Bears (stegó) All Things

Means to place under a roof, to cover over (with a roof), (figuratively) to endure because shielded, i.e., bearing up (forbearing) because under the Lor''s protection (covering).

The next four characteristics of agape each use the phrase "all things." The meaning from Bible Hub is: (The emphasis of the total picture then is on "one piece at a time" 365 (ananeóō) then focuses on the part(s) making up the whole – viewing the whole in terms of the individual parts.).

This is a sweeping statement. God's agape is directed outwardly toward all of His creation and every individual aspect of it. It is directed toward all of mankind and toward each individual human.

More specifically, the idea is that God bears, believes, hopes and endures with both the totality of our sin and each individual sin. This idea is captured in the old hymn "It is well with my soul": "My sin, oh, the bliss of this glorious thought! My sin, not in part but the whole, Is nailed to the cross, and I bear it no more. Praise the Lord, praise the Lord, o my soul!"

These four aspects of God's agape are all-inclusive. All things are actually only one Greek word translated as all. Literally, Love bears all. It leaves no room for exceptions.

God's agape love is bearing, covering or carrying all of mankind's fallenness. It reflects John the Baptist's words, "behold the lamb of God who takes away the sins of the world". (John 1:29). In Christ, God's agape has entered creation and is bearing or covering all the sins of all men. His love is protecting mankind as a whole and each person individually from their own self destruction.

Love Believes (pisteuó) all Things, Meaning believe, have faith in, and trust in.

This is an interesting concept. Agape love is reflected in belief or faith. What does that tell us about God, who is agape? The love of God always believes. Believes what? Meditate on this. God knows that no matter what circumstances we are in, no matter how dark our lives have become, His perfect love will find victory. He knows the infinite power of His love at work in us will be victorious: 100% victorious. His agape is for all mankind, and He "trusts" (knows) it will overcome the fall of creation and its curse.

Love Hopes(elpizó) All Things

Meaning actively waiting for God's fulfillment about the faith He has birthed through the power of His love (cf. Gal 5:6 with Heb 11:1) (Bible Hub)

The Biblical concept of hope is not a wish but an assured expectancy. It is the assured expectancy that our desire to see God's love in victory over fallen mankind will, at the appointed time, be fulfilled. We can look at those we know who are hopelessly lost in their sin, believing with an assured expectancy in the power of God's love.

Love Endures (hupomenó) All Things.

Meaning literally, remaining under (the load), bearing up (enduring) (Bible Hub)

God's love will never buckle under the weight of our sin. We can never be so lost that He pulls away His love. No matter what has happened, no matter how many times you've fallen, no matter how rebellious your heart may be, God's love for you never wavers. It never says you've had enough chances; I'm done. God is agape, and agape endures in all things and through all things to infinity and beyond, to quote the famous words of Buzz Lightyear.

Love Never Ends (piptó)

Meaning I fall, fall under (as under condemnation), fall prostrate (Bible Hub)

This is like the exclamation point, the AMEN, that follows a declaration of praise. It is typically translated agape never fails or never ends. Both are true but I think never fails is the better choice. Of course, it is true that agape never ends because it is an attribute of God's eternal nature. It cannot end. But what is being announced here is that God's agape love for mankind cannot fail. It will always and forever be at work in His relationship with mankind, and what love intends to accomplish will never fail.

Conclusions on God's love

The ultimate assurance of these 16 aspects of love is that through the cross, God's love for mankind cannot end in failure of any kind. All the enemies of love will be vanquished. Their power to destroy will be stripped away by agape. The breadth and power of God's love cannot be overestimated.

Immediately after giving us the opportunity to peer into the vastness of these 16 aspects of God's perfect love, Paul then says: *"For now we see in a mirror dimly, but then face to face. Now I know in part; then I shall know fully, even as I have been fully known."* (1 Corinthians 13:12 ESV). It is as if He is saying, I have opened a peephole to allow you to get a glimpse of God, but I want to remind you that in this life, we will only see a dim reflection of Him. He is so much greater than what Paul has described in these 16 aspects of love. This is why Paul prayed an amazing prayer for the church in Ephesians 3:14-21.

The text from this passage follows. Read it slowly and think about what Paul is saying about God's love:

14. For this reason I bow my knees before the Father, 15. from whom every family in heaven and on earth is named, 16. that according to the riches of his glory he may grant you to be strengthened with power through his Spirit in your inner being, 17. so that **Christ may dwell in your hearts through faith—that you, being rooted and grounded in love, 18. may have strength to comprehend with all the saints what is the breadth and length and height and depth, 19. and to know the love of Christ that surpasses knowledge, that you may be filled with all the fullness of God**.

20. Now to him who is able to do far more abundantly than all that we ask or think, according to the power at work within us, 21. to him be glory in the church and in Christ Jesus throughout all generations, forever and ever. Amen. (Eph 3:14-21 ESV)

Even though Paul readily admits that, at best, we can only see God's love dimly through these human eyes, he also prays that we might discern that love with our "spiritual" eyes to the degree that it fills our lives. Discerning God's nature and, specifically, God's love is not a theological exercise. It is the experience of Christ in your heart, manifesting Himself to you through your trust in Him (John 14:21). In all 16 aspects of love found in I Corinthians 13, Christ is revealing His love to you. When we, by faith, hold fast to what Paul is saying about God's love, the Spirit of Christ in us expands our concept of love and our ability to experience it.

May I encourage you to dig deeply into these verses in I Corinthians 13 with a heart believing that you are looking at the nature of Christ's love? And then talk with Him and ask Him to wipe a little more of the dust off your heart's mirror so that Christ might manifest more of His nature in you. This is the path, the only path, to spiritual growth. It is one hundred percent relational and it centers on burying yourself, by faith, inside of His nature and allowing Him to show you reality as He sees it and to respond as He would respond.

Meditate on these 16 characteristics of love and ask God to reveal more of His love to you. The more we understand the utter perfection of His love, the deeper our ability to trust Him in all His ways will grow. It is His perfect love that casts out all our fears (I Jn 4:18). In His love, there can be no foothold for fear and no room for doubt.

Part 8 – God Is Righteous and Just
(Ps 11:7)

Rest assured: Before God, the righteousness of Christ is all we need; before God, the righteousness of Christ is all we have.

Tullian Tchividjian

Deuteronomy 32:4 ESV "The Rock, his work is perfect, for all his ways **are justice**. A God of faithfulness and without iniquity, just and upright is he.

Ps 11:7 For the Lord **is righteous**; he loves righteous deeds; the upright shall behold his face.

Ps 145:17 ESV The Lord **is righteous** in all his ways and kind in all his works.

Romans 3:21 ESV But now the **righteousness** of God has been manifested apart from the law, although the Law and the Prophets bear witness to it—

Romans 1:17 ESV For in [the gospel], the **righteousness** of God is revealed from faith for faith, as it is written, "The righteous shall live by faith."

II Cor. 5:21 ESV For our sake, he made him to be sin who knew no sin so that in him we might become the **righteousness** of God.

Phil. 3:9 ESV and be found in him, not having a **righteousness** of my own that comes from the law, but that which comes through faith in Christ, the **righteousness** from God that depends on faith.

Read these seven verses again, but this time, read them as if they were one continuous paragraph. What do you see?

When we look at God's righteousness, we find the unfolding narrative of the gospel of our salvation. By faith, God is giving His own righteousness to us. As we trust Him, He gives us more and more of Himself. The gift of His righteousness is our only hope of healing from our inner brokenness and sin.

It was during this morning's devotion, while in the middle of developing this section on God's righteousness that Ps.119:149 (ESV) caught my eye: *"Hear* *my voice according to your steadfast love; O LORD, **according to your justice give me life.**"*

The verse highlights an idea that is important to consider as we transition from God's love to His righteousness. His love and His righteousness are in a partnership. The Psalmist understood them to be two sides of the same coin. It is because of God's steadfast love that He will always respond in a way that is right and just. He will respond in a way that brings life. If God is love, His justice must always seek to give life. Why? As we discussed in the prior section, that is how agape responds. It seeks to serve your greatest need.

God's justice is seen both in judgment and in grace, and it always comes to us wrapped in agape. We can rejoice in God, knowing that every member of the human race will one day come face to face with His righteousness. And we can trust Him in that moment, knowing that His love and righteousness will be victorious.

The words righteousness and justice combined are used a total of 675 times in scripture. Everything about God is right. He is just in every way. There is no possibility of a mistake with God. The creation and the ongoing development of His universe is flawless, and it is moving toward its intended destiny in every detail. That destiny will be a perfect reflection of His essential nature within the material world. His righteousness is making the universe right. He is reconciling creation to Himself (Col. 1:20).

The righteousness of God holds a special meaning for followers of Christ. It is described as a breastplate over our hearts protecting us from the evil of this world (Ephesians 6:14). It is a gift in response to a believer's faith that replaces our unrighteousness (Phil. 3:8,9; Rom. 1:17). It is a garment we wear that will ultimately obliterate our internal struggle with sin (Is. 61:10). It is clothing ourselves with Christ, who is our righteousness (Gal. 3:27; Rom. 13:14; 2 Cor.1:30). His righteousness includes everything we need.

It's easy to think of God's righteousness as a standard against which we are judged. But that's not the nature of His righteousness. His righteousness, or rightness, guides His relational love. His righteousness is for you, not against you. Everything about His relationship with you and His love for you is right. He will always respond to each human being righteously, in oneness with agape.

He knows what is right and will always do what is right. But it's greater than that. He doesn't just act righteous; He is righteous. Rightness is an aspect of His essential nature. That means there are no moral dilemmas in the mind of God. There is a perfect understanding of what is right that will always be reflected in all that He is and all that He does. This gives us reason to rejoice in all things, even in life's trials and disappointments. He is right there with us, responding in the right way so that His righteousness might grow in us.

We struggle at times with uncertainty about the right thing to do. Sometimes we are uncertain about how to do the right thing in the right way. But God does not experience this type of ethical dilemma. There's never a time when love demands one action, but righteousness demands another. We may lack the wisdom to understand what is both right and motivated by love. But there is no possibility of this happening within the oneness of God's nature. Why not?

Because God doesn't just choose to act righteously or to love; He is righteous, and He is love. They are both aspects of His essential nature. Even God's judgment of sinners is an act of His righteous love. This truth should bring immense comfort when our thoughts turn to family and friends who have died in unbelief. God's judgment is as much an act of love as is His forgiveness. His every action is perfect, it is right and it is motivated by love.

I understand you may find this hard to believe, especially when you read about His judgments in scripture. But to think of God in any other way is to impose our limitations onto His perfect nature. Our goal is to become more like Him. It is not to portray Him with human weakness and limitations. We have moral dilemmas, not God. We sometimes compromise what is right for the sake of love or vice versa. And we may not know how to love a seriously broken person. But God never has a hint of this type of moral conflict in His nature. His love and His righteousness always walk hand in hand.

I praise you, Lord, for the gift of your unchanging righteousness extended to all mankind. May the eyes of my heart see You as You are and reflect your goodness in this fallen world.

Part 9 – God Is Without Limits
(Is 43:13; Matt. 19:26; Job 42:1,2; Luke 1:37)

If God would concede to me His omnipotence for 24 hours, you would see how many changes I would make in the world. But if He gave me His wisdom, too, I would leave things as they are.

Jacques-Marie-Louis Monsabre Luke 1:37 ESV
For nothing will be impossible with God.

God's abilities have no limitations. There is nothing that He desires that He cannot accomplish. However, it is important to distinguish between His temporal desires and eternal desires. For example, God desires that all men would be righteous and walk in love. And yet, in this world, that desire remains unfulfilled. All men are not righteous, and even the best human effort to love falls short.

While this is true, it is also true that human "freedom of choice" can never interfere with the eternal plans of God. The limitations we place on God in this life are simply temporal manmade delusions. There is nothing that mankind can do, no stubborn rebellion we can throw in His face, that will alter or derail His eternal purposes.

In this section, we will consider three aspects of God's limitless nature:

A. His omniscience – Unlimited knowledge and understanding
B. His omnipotence – Unlimited power
C. His omnipresence – Unlimited presence within His creation

There is no possible way that man can thwart the eternal purposes of God. All our uncertainties and fears can be entrusted to Him. Why? His purposes for you are always motivated by His love, guided by His unlimited understanding, accomplished through His unbounded power and fulfilled by His continual presence in us. Take a few moments to reflect on these three aspects of God's nature in the following scriptures and capture your thoughts in the margins:

Eyes On God

A. His unlimited knowledge and understanding.
   i. Psalm 147:5–
      Great is our Lord and mighty in power; his understanding has **no limit.**
   ii. 1 John 3:20–
      If our hearts condemn us, we know that God is greater than our hearts, and he knows **everything**.
   iii. Psalm 139:4–
      Before a word is on my tongue, you, Lord, know it **completely**.
   iv. Hebrews 4:13–
      Nothing in all creation **is hidden** from God's sight. Everything is uncovered and laid bare before the eyes of him to whom we must give account.
   v. Isaiah 40:28–
      Do you not know?
      Have you not heard?
      The Lord is the everlasting God,
      the Creator of the ends of the earth.
      He will not grow tired or weary,
      and his understanding **no one can fathom**.

B. His unlimited power.
   i. Daniel 4:35–
      All the peoples of the earth are regarded as nothing.
      He does as he pleases
      with the powers of heaven and the peoples of the earth.
      No one can hold back his hand
      or say to him: "What have you done?"
   ii. Isaiah 14:27–
      For the Lord Almighty has purposed, and **who can thwart him**?
      His hand is stretched out, and who can turn it back?
   iii. Job 42:1,2–
      Then Job replied to the LORD:
      "I know that you **can do all things**;
      no purpose of yours can be thwarted.

iv.   Genesis 18:14–

Is anything too hard for the Lord? I will return to you at the appointed time next year, and Sarah will have a son."

v.   Luke 1:37–

For **nothing will be impossible** with God.

C.   His unlimited presence within creation.

iv.   Proverbs 15:3–
The eyes of the Lord are **everywhere**, keeping watch on the wicked and the good.

ii.   I Kings 8:27–
"But will God really dwell on the earth? The heavens, even the highest heaven, **cannot contain you**. How much less this temple I have built!

iii.   Jeremiah 23:23,24–
"Am I only a God nearby," declares the Lord,
"and not a God far away?
Who can hide in secret places so that I cannot see them?"
declares the Lord.
"**Do not I fill heaven and earth**?" declares the Lord.

iv.   Psalm 139:7-12–
Where can I go from your Spirit?
Where can I flee from your presence? If I go up to the heavens, **you are there**;
if I make my bed in the depths, **you are there**.
If I rise on the wings of the dawn,
if I settle on the far side of the sea, **even there, your hand will guide me**, your right hand will hold me fast.

If I say, "Surely the darkness will hide me, and the light become night around me," **even the darkness will not be dark to you**; the night will shine like the day, for darkness is as light to you.

v.   Colossians 1:17–

He is before all things, and in him all things hold together.

God is perpetually present in every place and every time in the universe. At this very moment, His presence is with me as I fly over northern Florida. His presence is with every person on the planet. In fact, His presence is with every atom in the created universe and in every moment across creation's timeline.

This does not mean that God is so big; He fills space and time. It is not about His size. He is an infinite, unbounded spirit. He created space, matter and time, but these do not define or limit His abilities because He, as Spirit, is Holy and separate from creation. God is fully present, with no distraction of any kind, in every relationship, in every location, at every moment. All of His attention is always focused on you, and nothing can interrupt that attention. And yet He is simultaneously focusing on billions of others around the planet, across history and to the end of time (if there is such a thing). Add to that the fact that it is His presence that actively holds the universe together (Col. 1:17). And finally, He is not present as a casual observer but as an active participant moving His creation toward complete reconciliation (Col. 1:20).

As difficult as it is to understand the idea of being present everywhere, the notion that He is present in every moment of time is even more jaw-dropping. He is the alpha and omega. He is present across the entire timeline, beginning to end. It's not that He was present in the past; he is present in the current moment and will be present in the future. God is the great I AM. The timeline is His creation. He is present in time, holding it together as He holds the universe together. Just as He is always present in every place in the universe He is also always present in every time.

God is in our tomorrow before tomorrow comes. He owns time. The future is His creation, not simply the result of mankind's freedom of choice.

It is God's omnipresence that defines the context in which His knowledge and power operate. Wherever God's unbounded presence is found, there we also find His unlimited power guided by perfect knowledge and wisdom. The implications are staggering. God's unlimited power is simultaneously and perpetually at work everywhere in the universe and in every moment, from the Garden of Eden to the new heavens and new earth.

From our temporal perspective, God appears to have limitations. We may wonder how it is possible an all-powerful God of love could allow such horrific suffering in this world. Isn't this strong evidence that God is unable to stop human misery? And so we conclude that God's abilities are limited. He must lack the ability or the desire to respond. We conclude that His power, His love, or possibly His understanding, is lacking. But this is simply finite human reasoning.

In Romans 8, the apostle Paul redirects our thoughts to an eternal perspective. Think about his inspired words:

18 For I consider that the sufferings of this present time are not worth comparing with the glory that is to be revealed to us. 19 For the creation waits with eager longing for the revealing of the sons of God. 20 For the creation was subjected to futility, not willingly, but because of him who subjected it, in hope 21 that the creation itself will be set free from its bondage to corruption and obtain the freedom of the glory of the children of God. 22 For we know that the whole creation has been groaning together in the pains of childbirth until now. 23 And not only the creation, but we ourselves, who have the first fruits of the Spirit, groan inwardly as we wait eagerly for adoption as sons, the redemption of our bodies. 24 For in this hope we were saved. Now hope that is seen is not hope.

For who hopes for what he sees? 25 But if we hope for what we do not see, we wait for it with patience. (Romans 8:18-27 ESV).

As Paul anticipates the unfolding eternal plan of God, he concludes that the suffering of this age cannot be compared to what that suffering is producing in us. He compares creation to a woman giving birth to a child. Creation is the womb from which a reconciled humanity will emerge. That which is temporal gives birth to the eternal.

It is impossible to understand the limitless nature of God from a temporal perspective. It's like an unborn child wondering if mommy knows what she is doing. The temporal universe is like a mother's womb, a place of development. It is a place from which a new creation will be given birth. It is in bondage to corruption, but that corruption actually serves an eternal purpose. The suffering of this age is designed to set the children of God free. We must look beyond this present age to understand the unlimited nature of God.

Evil and suffering both exist in this temporal age by God's design. While God is not the author of evil, His nature does permit evil in the temporal realm but never in the eternal. That was the point of not allowing Adam and Eve to eat from the Tree of Life in the Garden of Eden (Genesis 3:22-24). Evil and rebellion will never enter the eternal realm. Evil must be exposed and dealt with as a temporal concern so that the things that are passing away might be made incorruptible.

This is the context in which we say that God has no limits. There are no limits to His power (omnipotent), no limits to His knowledge (omniscient), and no limits to His access (omnipresent in both time and space). He has all power, knowledge and understanding over every aspect of the entire universe, both past, present and future. Everything about God is working in creation, moving it toward the day of total reconciliation (Col. 1:20). Knowing that He is without limitation is our assured hope that the promised day will come.

When I make the statement, "There is nothing God desires that He cannot accomplish," I mean there is nothing God desires in His temporal creation that He will not accomplish in eternity. It is not a promise for this passing world. It is a promise to which this world will give birth.

God's temporal will, which permits evil and suffering, is accomplishing His eternal plan. It is toward this end that His wisdom, power and presence are at work in our lives. Our faith unites with this reality, and we know there is nothing in this universe that will ever stand between us and the goodness of God. The things that cause us to question God in this life are exactly what we need to prepare us for eternity. And the process will continue until we are shaped into a perfect reflection of Christ.

There has been a fairly recent attack on God's unlimited nature from a theological framework known as open theology. Open theology has grown in popularity over the last 25-30 years. The movement gained momentum in 1994 when five evangelical scholars - David Basinger, William Hasker, Clark Pinnock, Richard Rice, and John Sanders – published "The Openness of God: A Biblical Challenge to the Traditional Understanding of God."

At its core, open theology presents a new model for understanding God's knowledge-a model that insists that genuine human freedom requires that God cannot know human decisions in advance. They reason that if God knows our choices in advance, then freedom of choice cannot be genuine. This idea is a manmade limitation placed on God by human logic, not the scriptures. It is a theological idea that is an open denial of God's omniscience and places God on creation's timeline, waiting with mankind to see what choices we will make and then deciding how He will respond. It is a dangerous projection of human limitations onto the nature of God.

Open theology is an example of a recent construct that has tried to strip God of his omniscience over the future. It attacks the scriptural teaching that God, who is eternal, is not constrained by temporal things such as time or space.

Open theology literally takes an aspect of God's creation, the future, and claims that it has some form of power over Him. He cannot really know the future because the decisions of men are what determine the future, not God. Not only does He have no authority over the future, but He cannot even know in what direction the decisions of men will take the future.

In open theology, man decides, and God reacts. Having a clear understanding of the nature of God can protect us from man-centric ideas like this that distort God's essential nature.

If our understanding of God's nature is muddled, we become an easy target for false teaching. Doubts about God will quickly cloud our thinking and lead us astray from the clear teaching of scripture. Living life in this temporal world will make no sense until it is viewed from the perspective of the eternal. To reverse the order and try to understand an eternal God from the perspective of the natural world is a fool's errand. The result will always be an idol made in our own image.

I understand that when we see the dysfunction of this world, it appears that mankind is running roughshod over the purposes and goodness of God. Human reasoning will always lead us to this conclusion. Yet God, who possesses the power to call the universe into existence out of nothing, also has the ability to accomplish whatever He pleases within that universe.

There is nothing His creation could possibly do to thwart His purpose. There is no possibility that God could ever have a desire against which any created thing could ever stand. Yes, His creation is in discord with His purposes.

But that discord, while permitted as an element of His plan, cannot continue into the eternal state. His plan is a complete reconciliation, and His power will continue to be exerted on creation until it is accomplished.

At best, the only thing men can see in this world is a snapshot in time from which we draw conclusions about God. But we do this from a very limited perspective. God's power does not flow into creation in reaction to events as they unfold. It may appear that way to us, but God is eternal. Because God is eternal, His influence on His creation flows out of eternity. God's wisdom, power, and presence within His creation have no possible constraints other than being consistent with His essential nature.

This tells us that the relational God of infinite, unfailing love has the power, wisdom and access to His creation necessary to fulfill His good and perfect desires. This truth is inscrutable. Though we can't understand it, we cling to Him by faith, knowing that He is able to do what He has promised. And by His promises, our souls are refreshed in our daily walk with Him.

Fix your eyes on Him!

SECTION 3 - GOD'S NATURE MADE KNOWN IN CHRIST

He that made man was made man.

C. H. Spurgeon

*John 1:1-18 **1** In the beginning was the **Word**, and the **Word** was with God, and the **Word** was God. **2** He was in the beginning with God. **3** All things were made through him, and without him was not any thing made that was made. **4** In him was life, and the life was the light of men. **5** The light shines in the darkness, and the darkness has not overcome it.*

*__**6** There was a man sent from God, whose name was John. **7** He came as a witness, to bear witness about the light, that all might believe through him. **8** He was not the light, but came to bear witness about the light.__*

*__**9** The true light, which gives light to everyone, was coming into the world. **10** He was in the world, and the world was made through him, yet the world did not know him. **11** He came to his own, and his own people did not receive him.__*

*__**12** But to all who did receive him, who believed in his name, he gave the right to become children of God, **13** who were born, not of blood nor of the will of the flesh nor of the will of man, but of God.__*

*__**14** And the **Word became flesh and dwelt among us, and we have seen his glory, glory as of the only Son from the Father**, full of grace and truth.__*

*__**15** (John bore witness about him, and cried out, "This was he of whom I said, 'He who comes after me ranks before me, because he was before me.'") **16** For from his fullness we have all received, grace upon grace. **17** For the law was given through Moses; grace and truth came through Jesus Christ. **18** No one has ever seen God; the only God, who is at the Father's side, he has made him known.__*

The Greek word Logos translates to "the word" in English. It is a common Greek word meaning to express our thoughts and our reasoning. In scripture, the term is frequently used to describe an expression of God. It represents the mind of God as it is being opened to our hearts by the Holy Spirit. The Word is an expression of who God really is. It shows us the nature of God.

The Word of God has similarities to our spoken word, but it communicates infinitely more. Our words reveal what is in our hearts, as seen in Luke 6:45: "... Out of the abundance of the heart the mouth speaks". Likewise, the Word of God reflects God's heart to His creation.

We often refer to the Bible as the Word of God, but that is not technically correct. The Bible reveals the Word to us. The actual Word of God is living. It is the infinite Holy nature of God. It cannot be contained in the Bible's pages. The Word of God became flesh in Christ and revealed God's essential nature to us (see John 1:14 above). Literally, the Word of God is the nature of God being gifted to us in the birth, the life, and the death of Jesus.

The Word became flesh in a virgin's womb. The Holy Spirit brought the Holy nature of God into human flesh. The nature of God dwelt among us in the form of a man.

This is why the virgin birth is so important. Jesus is not the best the human race has to offer. He is the arrival of the nature of the unseen God in the form of an embryo found in a virgin's womb. Mary was chosen and blessed by God so that He might give Himself to mankind, untouched by the sin of this world. And it is God's plan to reconcile His fallen creation to Himself through that gift (Col 1:20). We know this gift as Jesus the Messiah, the Son of the living God.

This life that was placed in Mary's womb is pure and unblemished. It is the gift of perfect love.

At the moment the Holy Spirit brought life into Mary's womb, a new creation was initiated. The first Adam was formed from the dust of the earth. The second Adam (the man Jesus) was formed from the breath of Heaven. The nature of God took up residence in creation. God took on human form. Yet, in every way, Jesus was Holy, separate from creation.

This is why Jesus declared His self-existence by saying, "Before Abraham was born, I am." in John 8:58. The Jewish leaders of His day recognized this as a claim to self-existence, which was a claim only God could make. Jesus is self-existent. He is Holy with no dependency on creation for anything. He is the beginning of a new creation. His existence does not depend on the natural process of human conception. And yet, from the moment of conception until His death, He submitted to the processes of normal human existence, experiencing our joy and our pain and even enduring the suffering of the cross.

The self-existent God, in Christ, has physically entered creation. Because He is not limited by time and is always fully present in every place, there is never a moment when He is not with us. In fact, He has been in our darkest days long before we experience them. The breath of Heaven has walked where you have walked. He is walking where you are now. And He has already walked in your future. To say He dwells with us means that He perpetually dwells in the entire timeline of your existence. In every moment of our lives we are being shaped by the one who knows the beginning from the end and whose love can never fail. This incomprehensible gift should cast our fears far from us.

Romans 8:15 (ESV) *For you did not receive the spirit of slavery to fall back into fear, but you have received the Spirit of adoption as sons, by whom we cry, "Abba! Father!"*

In chapter 14 of the Gospel of John, while Jesus was teaching His disciples, Philip asked Him to "show us the Father." In other words, he was saying, "We would like to meet God the Father. Can you please arrange a get-together?". Jesus responded to Philip with a very pointed question. Here is the passage:

John 14:5-10 (ESV)

5 Thomas said to him, "Lord, we do not know where you are going. How can we know the way?" 6 Jesus said to him, "I am the way, and the truth, and the life.

No one comes to the Father except through me. 7 If you had known me, you would have known my Father also. From now on you do know him and have seen him."

*8 Philip said to him, "**Lord, show us the Father**, and it is enough for us."*

*9 Jesus said to him, "**Have I been with you so long, and you still do not know me, Philip? Whoever has seen me has seen the Father. How can you say, 'Show us the Father?' 10 Do you not believe that I am in the Father*** *and the Father is in me? The words that I say to you I do not speak on my own authority, but the Father who dwells in me does his works.*

Jesus was challenging Philip's thinking about God. Why do you ask to see the Father? When you see me you are seeing all that the Father is. In Christ, there is no aspect of the Father's nature lacking. Jesus is the exact image of His Father. All of the nature of God is seen in Jesus (Hebrews 1:3; Colossians 1:15).

But there is an unexpected twist to this story that we discover in Phil 2:

6 [Jesus], though he was in the form of God, did not count equality with God a thing to be grasped, 7 but emptied himself, by taking the form of a servant, being born in the likeness of men. Phil 2:6,7 (ESV)

This passage is known as the kenosis (the act of emptying) of Christ. He emptied Himself of some aspects or privileges of deity when He became a man. Why would He do this? The Old Testament story of Moses sheds some light on why this was necessary:

*18 Then Moses said, "Now, please show me your glory (**Who you are, your essential nature**)."*

*19 The Lord answered, "I will cause all my goodness to pass in front of you, and I will announce my name, the Lord, so you can hear it. I will show kindness to anyone to whom I want to show kindness, and I will show mercy to anyone to whom I want to show mercy. 20 But you cannot see my face, because **no one can see me and live.** Exodus 33:18-20 (ESV)*

Jesus is all that God is. God's nature [glory] is fully present in Him, and He took on flesh so that we might see the nature of God in physical form. However, we could not survive a direct exposure to the fullness of God's nature, so Christ willingly set aside any aspect of His deity that could harm His creation. When He became flesh, He emptied Himself and became a reflection of God's nature that would benefit us. Everything we witnessed about Jesus is a perfect reflection of the nature of God, but we did not see all that God is. That would have destroyed mankind. So, while Jesus is the exact image of God (Colossians 1:15; Hebrews 1:3), He willingly emptied Himself of any aspect of deity that would not advance the purposes of God during His time with us on earth.

This act of humility, known as the kenosis or emptying of Christ's glory to fulfill the redemptive purposes of the Father, is an incomprehensible reality. Love always sets aside its self-interests to meet the needs of others. But to set aside the glory of God to become a servant to His own creation, knowing all the while He would be rejected and ultimately crucified, is just crazy. If this is true, and it certainly is, how could we ever question the love of God? His love is beyond our imagination.

There was only one way to meet our need for healing and forgiveness. It was the Kenosis. The devil's temptation in the wilderness was to entice Jesus to question His Father and to take back the glory that He had set aside (Matthew 4:1-11). The devil was looking for a weakness in the love of God. He could not believe that the Word of God would willingly empty Himself. He could not fathom a love that powerful. He miscalculated, and so do we when we place limits on the love of God.

Our creator set aside some aspect of His glory and became a servant, which in itself is a miracle, to demonstrate His love for us and to offer us forgiveness. He then allowed His creation to abuse Him, to mock Him and to ultimately crucify Him. Love emptied itself and died so that we might live.

This poses an interesting question. If Jesus emptied Himself of some aspects of being God in order to become a servant, wouldn't He be something less than the Father? And how can Jesus say, "If you've seen me, you've seen the Father" if He had emptied Himself when He became a man?

Everything the disciples saw and heard in Jesus was a perfect reflection of God's nature in action. They saw God's nature at work in the necessary way to reach their hearts. To be exposed to all that God is would have destroyed them.

Jesus revealed to us what God is like so that we can become like Him in our relationships. His self-revelation is not a theology lesson. It is a relationship lesson. The disciples saw the Father's perfect relational love in Jesus. And when we see His perfect love through faith, we too can walk in this world like Jesus walked.

Jesus has set aside or veiled the glory of being God so that His perfect love can be made known on earth.

John 3:16 (ESV) - *"For God so loved the world, that he gave his only Son, that whoever believes in him should not perish but have eternal life."*

Are there fears or anxieties that haunt you and rob you of inner peace?

Remember this:

Jesus has already **walked through** your entire life's experience. How do I know this? Because He is always present across time and space.

Isaiah 46:10 (ESV)

declaring the end from the beginning and from ancient times things not yet done, saying, 'My counsel shall stand, and I will accomplish all my purpose

Jesus has already **worked through** your entire life's experience. How do I know this? Because His love never fails, and there are no limits to His ability.

Romans 8:28 (ESV)

And we know that for those who love God all things work together for good, for those who are called according to his purpose.

Jesus has already **accomplished His purpose through** your entire life's experience. How do I know this? Because His sovereign purposes cannot be thwarted.

Phil 1:6 (ESV)

he who began a good work in you will bring it to completion at the day of Jesus Christ.

And do this:

I Peter 5:7 (ESV)

cast all your anxieties on him, because he cares for you

Matt 11:29 (ESV)

Take my yoke upon you, and learn from me, for I am gentle and lowly in heart, and you will find rest for your souls.

As you reflect deeply on His nature, He will begin to cast out all your fears and draw you into the experience of His perfect love that sets us free.

SECTION 4 - TRUSTING GOD'S NATURE

Never be afraid to trust an unknown future to a known God.

Corrie Ten Boom

Ps 31:14 But I trust in you, O Lord; I say, "You are my God." (ESV)

In the previous sections, we discussed the unfathomable vastness of God's nature, looking for insight into who God is and what He is really like. In this section, we will look at why having clarity about God's nature and trusting Him is so important in a believer's life.

Any addict who has participated in a 12-step recovery program recognizes that the success of the program is built on the idea of trusting God or some higher power. There is incredible dysfunction in this world, and many people eventually realize they can't control their own lives. Difficult circumstances and events outside of our control make us feel vulnerable at best. When things get really bad, we feel broken and helpless. The Psalmist says in Ps 31 that he trusts in the Lord. The addict is encouraged to trust in God as He understands Him.

Most of us have some concept of a higher power to bring a little stability and sanity to our lives. The question is: "What is that higher power really like?". The answer to that question will be the foundation on which we build our lives. It will be the thing (or person) in which we trust. The Psalmist chose to trust His creator. It makes sense to trust the one who cared enough to create you, understands your purpose, and intimately knows you. Christians want to know their creator, and they turn to scripture to answer the question, "What is God really like?"

The purpose of knowing what God is like is to assure us that we are trusting God for who He really is. Our Christian growth depends on it. Everything God does in the temporal universe is consistent with, motivated by and a perfect reflection of all nine characteristics of God's essential nature, which we have studied. In this section, we will briefly look at how they shape our concept of God and their importance in our spiritual development.

God is Self-Existent

The source and motivation for every action God takes originates outside of fallen creation. Creation itself bears the stamp of God's nature, but sin has distorted its perfection. We saw, in Section 2 Part 7 on God is Love, that the source of sin actually originates within the nature of God's love, which allows independence and freedom of choice for His creatures. God's perfect love made sin possible and possibly even inevitable. Because of this, sin became the tragic result of God's love. However, sin is not a reflection of some flaw in God's nature. It is a temporal problem, not an eternal reality.

The message of the gospel is that because of man's sin, God responded in love and creation began a transformation in Christ that will result in its complete reconciliation to God, and it will ultimately, in the eternal state, perfectly reflect the nature of God. While it's true that God's love permitted sin (Agape does not insist on its own way - I Cor. 13:4,5), it is also true that His love never gives up and it never fails (I Col 13:8). Reconciliation, not sin, is the end of the story.

It is the self-existent nature of God's love that assured Paul that the fallen creation is being drawn into perfect reconciliation and harmony with Him. His creative work is not complete until all created things have been reconciled to Him, "making peace by the blood of His cross" (Col 1:20). It is then, and only then, that the universe will perfectly manifest the nature of God. And because of His self-existence, that day is a certainty.

It is God's self-existence that reassures us that God is not like this fallen creation. We can rest assured that His actions will never be governed by rules that reflect the problems and issues we face in this fallen world. His actions are always a perfect and complete reflection of His self-existent nature apart from this world.

When we are tempted to think of God in human terms, remember that God is self-existent. What He is like cannot be discerned from the perspective of this fallen creation. We can only trust what He has revealed about His nature in scripture and then look at the world in which we live through that lens. Trusting Him for who He really is the essence of our faith. It allows us to see God's creation through His eyes. **We can trust God's self-revelation in Scripture.**

God is Holy

There is no possibility that anything could ever tarnish God's character. Creation responds to His perfect desires and can never corrupt His goodness. **We can trust that there is no possible flaw in God.**

God is One

God is not a blend of attributes. His oneness means 100 percentness. I realize that percentness is not a real word, but the nature of God is 100% of everything He is. The danger of looking at different aspects of God's character is that we start to think of them as separate elements of His nature. They are not. God is one. **You can trust that everything God does will perfectly reflect everything that God is.**

God is Eternal

Eternal is not a time word. God created time; eternal is outside of time. It has more to do with the quality of existence than its duration. Creation is massive, but it has boundaries. It has a beginning and an end. There are limits on the character and duration of life. But none of creation's limitations or boundaries are found in the eternal nature of God. We should never place man-made boundaries on God. **You can trust that absolutely nothing in creation will ever limit God.**

God is Immutable

God's character cannot be corrupted, nor can it be improved. No amount of evil will ever tarnish His nature. His response to everything, including each of us, will always be a perfect and complete reflection of His oneness. You may fall from God's grace, but you will never fall from God's love. Remember, grace is God's response to repentance; it is not a characteristic of His nature. Grace is an action that depends on the situational circumstances. But love is the nature of God. It is immutable. **You can trust that God's nature is absolutely perfect, and nothing about it will ever change.**

God is Relational

You can be thankful that God is not an all-powerful, impersonal being. God is relational. This means much more than God has relationships. He Himself, by virtue of His nature, is a relationship. His nature defines perfect relationships. The gospel is an invitation to enter into that relationship.

Other aspects of God's nature help us understand His perfect relational nature. Perfect Relationship is:

1. Self-existing. We did not discover nor did God create relationships. They are self-existent in the nature of God.
2. Holy. Meaning it exists separate from fallen creation. We can only understand it by looking at God. A humanistic approach to relationships may provide some value, but it will always, at some point, fall short.
3. One. Meaning it reflects perfect unity. No conflict can exist in God's relational nature. Likewise, a perfect relationship cannot exist apart from God. The relational dysfunction of this world should be no surprise.
4. Eternal. Meaning it has no boundaries. There is nothing hidden or unknown that might damage a perfect relationship.
5. Immutable. Meaning in Christ there is no chance of a broken relationship.
6. Governed by perfect love. Meaning it completely reflects everything we learned about agape in I Corinthians 13.
7. Righteous and Just. Meaning goodness and truth are never compromised for the relationship's sake.
8. Without limits. Meaning that in Christ our relationships are built on His unlimited knowledge and understanding, His unlimited power, and His unlimited presence with us and His creation.

We cannot even begin to fathom what God can and will accomplish when all relationships are reconciled, restored and brought into unity with His nature. We should be eternally grateful that God is a relational God. Any concept of God that tampers with or minimizes His relational nature has failed to see God as He really is. **You can trust a relationship with Christ.**

God is Love

It is impossible for us to imagine the extent of infinite love. It is self-existent within the nature of a Holy God. But God has revealed that love in scripture and His Spirit has brought it experientially to life in the hearts of believers. As we see deeper into the nature of God's love, we are drawn into it. This is the very essence of a believer's spiritual growth. It is how we connect to Christ and grow in Him. We have observed a number of important things about the nature of God's love in the prior section. Meditate on the following summary of these ideas and let them push the boundaries of your understanding of God's love.

And then ask God for the grace needed to walk in that love. God's Love:

Is Slow to Anger - Even His anger is love. The purpose of His anger is to produce goodness in us.

Is Kind - Understands and serves our greatest needs

Does not Envy - It never desires to take from you to satisfy personal desires. God would never want you to suffer so He could settle some score with you.

Does not Boast - When we stand before God, He will not put on some display of how great He is. Love does not try to make you feel small and insignificant.

Is not rude - It does not offend and try to make you feel uncomfortable.

Does not insist on its own way - It does not force anyone into compliance. The idea of forced submission to God's will is a direct violation of the nature of love. The "do what I say or else" concept of God is a man-made construct.

Is not irritable - It never responds with a reactionary feelings-based type of anger.

It does not keep a record of wrongs - No matter how long the list of our sins has become, it is our list, not God's. To think that the evil in your heart has grown larger than God's love for you is idolatry.

It Does Not Rejoice at wrongdoing - While love does not keep a record of sin, it hates sin and the damage it causes.

It Rejoices with the Truth - It rejoices when sin is confessed and brought into the light. Love seeks healing, not retribution.

It bears All Things - In Christ, God's love bears or covers all the sins of all mankind.

It believes All Things - Perfect, infinite love is confident that it will ultimately overcome all sin in complete victory.

Hopes All Things - It is the assured expectancy that our desire to see God's love in victory over fallen mankind will, at the appointed time, be fulfilled.

Endures All Things - Perfect love never wavers. It is immutable.

Never Ends or Fails - Perfect love continues on, unbroken, undiminished, and its purposes will never fail.

You can trust that God's love for you is unbreakable and unfailing. Nothing in all of creation can ever separate you from His love (Romans 8:35-39).

God is Righteous

Everything about God is right. Righteousness informs and guides all His interactions with the human race. Believers are protected by His righteousness (Eph. 6:14). They are covered with everything that is right (Is. 61:10). Our flawed humanness is being replaced by His righteousness (Phil. 3:8,9; Rom. 1:17). **You can trust that God's righteousness will heal your brokenness and transform your character into a reflection of all that is right.**

God is without limits

God's unlimited wisdom and power are present and at work in every place and every moment within the universe. You can trust God to fulfill His perfect plan for your earthly life and your eternal existence.

These ideas are foundational in how we approach our relationship with God and His Word. Interpreting scripture in a way that is consistent with His Self-revelation will significantly enhance our walk with Him. Reading the Bible through the lens of God's essential nature has become the primary way that I approach the scriptures. In the next section I will draw examples from my personal journal entries and share how this has shaped my own understanding of scripture.

SECTION 5 - DISCOVERING GOD'S NATURE AT WORK IN SCRIPTURE

What God wants is to reveal himself more fully to us

Steven Curtis Chapman

In the previous sections we spent time clarifying what the nature of God is really like and what it means to trust His nature. In this section, we will look at a few selected scriptures through the lens of God's essential nature.

It is through scripture that we encounter the living Jesus. Fixing our eyes on His nature as we read the Bible should become a lifelong pattern for believers. The primary goal of scripture is not just to discover truth. It is to fall in love with the author of truth. Knowledge alone feeds our pride. It puffs up. But love builds up (I Cor. 8:1). Jesus said all of scripture hangs on love; on our love for God and our love for one another (Matt 22:36-40). The goal of scripture is totally relational. We go to scripture to discover and experience the love of God and then bring His love into this fallen world.

As you read scripture, if you find yourself coming to conclusions about the meaning of a passage that in any way casts a shadow of doubt across the goodness of God's nature, you should pray for an understanding that is more consistent with what you know to be true about God. To put it in other words, if it is a choice between protecting your theological ideas or protecting the nature of God, don't ever tamper with the nature of God.

In this section, I will share a selection of passages, some of which are difficult, and discuss how I approach them in light of God's nature. The idea of using God's nature as a filter is better caught than taught. So, the rest of this section will include a series of passages along with reflections I have developed using God's nature as a filter as I study the passages.

Just to be clear, I am not trying to do an in-depth exposition of these passages. This section is meant to illustrate how reading the scripture through the lens of God's nature can shape our understanding of its meaning. I should give a word of caution at this point. This is not a license to speculate and twist scripture's meaning into something that makes us comfortable. It should never preclude the proper study of language, culture and context. It is simply approaching the passage in a way that ensures our understanding remains faithful to the revealed nature of God.

I John 2:15 (ESV)

15 Do not love the world or the things in the world. For all that is in the world - the desires of the flesh and the desires of the eyes and the pride of life - Is not from the Father but is from the world.

Reflection:

The Greek word translated love is agape or perfect love. Agape involves a choice and a commitment. It is in a relationship with a perfect, unwavering commitment to the relationship. It is a relationship that we live for and for which we would die. God is agape, and in Christ, He lived and died for a relationship with us.

John is saying agape should have no connection with the things of this world. Everything about the world, including our flesh, is passing away. To love this world is to love death. Agape is a choice, and when the choice is made, the associated feelings from that choice will follow. The love of the world produces deeper and deeper feelings of lust, desire, greed and pride. The love of God produces deeper feelings of humility, kindness, gentleness, compassion and wisdom. What we love, we become.

Lord, help me focus my love on you alone.

I John 3:2,3 (ESV)

*2 Beloved, we are God's children now, and what we will be has not yet appeared; but we know that when He appears we shall be like Him, because we **shall see Him as He is. 3 And everyone who thus hopes in Him purifies himself** as He is pure*.

Reflection:

Our concept of God is what we are becoming. John equates our becoming like Him to seeing Him as He is. What will ultimately transform us is when we see Him as He is, with no shadow of doubt or confusion. The closer we come to seeing God's nature as it really is, especially His love, the greater our desire grows to love Him and others in the same manner. That's why Jesus said when we pursue love, He will manifest Himself to us (Jn 14:12). Our love can be no greater than our understanding and experience of His love.

He is agape. Everything He does is motivated by perfect love. To pursue love is to pursue Him as He really is.

A second idea comes from verse 3. It is my hope, or assured expectation, that when I do see Him clearly, as He is, I will become like Him. It is my hope that produces the desire and energy to fight against the love of this world (I Jn 2:15). When I look deeper into His amazing love, I remember His promise, and it gives me the energy to fight my pride and broken desires one more day. Who fights against the lusts of this world? Everyone who thus hopes in Him.

Q1 - What is it that produces my growth in love?

A1 - To see Him as He is. We grow by entering into God's nature.

Q2 - From where does my desire and energy to continually purify myself come?

A2 - My confident hope in the promise that I will one day be like Him.

I John 4:18,19 (ESV)

18 There is no fear in love, but perfect love casts out fear. For fear has to do with punishment, and whoever fears has not been perfected in love. 19 We love because He first loved us.

Reflection:

Fear can be paralyzing. The world is a dangerous place, and apart from the certainty that everything that touches this planet is guided by God's love, we would have legitimate reason to be overcome by fear. Fear, in fact, is the root cause of many anxiety disorders prevalent in our modern society.

Apart from God's love for me and all of creation, fear may be the only reasonable response to living in a fallen world.

Do you fear sickness and death? Do you fear pain and suffering? Do you fear rejection and abandonment? Do you fear evil? Do you fear job loss or a collapse of the stock market? Do you have friends or family who are ensnared in sin? Or even worse, who has died in unbelief? Do you fear the judgment they will face? Can you trust that every event in all of creation is guided by the perfect sovereign love of God? Do you place any limits on the active presence of God's love at work in any situation? Have you unknowingly refused to allow perfect love to cast out your fear?

Unfortunately, becoming a Christian does not automatically eliminate our fears. Christians struggle with many of the same fears as unbelievers. We taste perfect love in salvation, but we must grow in love relationally. Perfect love grows in us as we experience the nature of Christ's love for us and all creation.

I believe there is a simple test that can help each of us evaluate the growth of our experience in God's perfect love. There is a direct relationship between God's love at work in us and our fears. As our experience of God's love grows, the basis of our trust in Him grows, and our fears diminish. It is almost like a blood pressure test for our spiritual hearts. An increase in our fears is like high blood pressure. But there are no Beta Blocker pills for the soul. Only the knowledge and experience of the nature of God's love will drive out all our fears.

Lord, may the experience of your love in me drive out all the fears that have ensnared me.

Ps 5:5 (ESV)

5 The boastful cannot stand in Your presence; You hate all workers of iniquity

Ps 139: 21,22 (ESV)

21 Do I not hate those who hate you, O Lord? And do I not loathe those who rise up against you? 22 I hate them with complete hatred; I count them my enemies.

Reflection:

These two verses are often quoted as evidence that God does not love all mankind and that, in fact, he hates his enemies. In spite of the fact that the central message of scripture is the universal nature of God's love, some Calvinists use these verses to support the idea that God's perfect love is shown only to the elect and not all mankind. This is an egregious challenge against the nature of God.

The first thing to note is that hate is not an attribute of God. An enemy of God who repents and turns to Christ in faith is no longer hated. In fact, while we were still enemies, Christ died for us, demonstrating His love for his enemies. Love is always present in God. Hate is a transient thing.

We think of love and hate as opposites, like two sides of a teeter-totter. Our emotions swing back and forth between "love" and "hate" based on the circumstances. God is nothing like that.

The Hebrew word translated as hate is not a feeling word. It means to stand against a person. God totally, with no compromise, stands against those who are "workers of iniquity." It is nothing like our feelings-based concept of hatred. He is against them because they oppose His goodness. But He loves them, and that is why "while we were still sinners, Christ died for us" Rom. 5:8 (ESV).

God stands against His enemies because of His love for them.

Matt 25:31-46 (ESV)

31 "When the Son of Man comes in his glory, and all the angels with him, then he will sit on his glorious throne. 32 Before him will be gathered all the nations, and he will separate people one from another as a shepherd separates the sheep from the goats. 33 And he will place the sheep on his right, but the goats on the left. 34 Then the King will say to those on his right, 'Come, you who are blessed by my Father, inherit the kingdom prepared for you from the foundation of the world. 35

For I was hungry, and you gave me food, I was thirsty, and you gave me drink, I was a stranger, and you welcomed me, 36 I was naked, and you clothed me, I was sick, and you visited me, I was in prison, and you came to me.' 37 Then the righteous will answer him, saying, 'Lord, when did we see you hungry and feed you, or thirsty and give you drink? 38 And when did we see you a stranger and welcome you, or naked and clothe you? 39 And when did we see you sick or in prison and visit you?' 40 And the King will answer them, 'Truly, I say to you, as you did it to one of the least of these my brothers, [f] you did it to me.'

41 "Then he will say to those on his left, 'Depart from me, you cursed, into the eternal fire prepared for the devil and his angels. 42 For I was hungry, and you gave me no food, I was thirsty, and you gave me no drink, 43 I was a stranger, and you did not welcome me, naked and you did not clothe me, sick and in prison and you did not visit me.' 44 Then they also will answer, saying, 'Lord, when did we see you hungry or thirsty or a stranger or naked or sick or in prison, and did not minister to you?' 45 Then he will answer them, saying, 'Truly, I say to you, as you did not do it to one of the least of these, you did not do it to me.' 46 And these will go away into eternal punishment, but the righteous into eternal life."

Reflection:

This passage describes the separation of the sheep from the goats by Christ prior to His 1000-year earthly reign. The sheep are those who faithfully walk in God's love. The goats did not. Inherent in the Greek word for faith (pistis) is the idea of faithfulness. Saving faith produces faithfulness evident by love as seen in welcoming strangers, providing for the naked, the hungry, the thirsty and visiting the sick. In Rom. 1:5, the apostle Paul described it as "the obedience that comes from faith."

The faithful (those whose faith produced the fruit of obedience) went into "eternal life," and the unfaithful went to "eternal punishment." We can easily see the love of God at work as He shows grace to the sheep in this passage. But we struggle with seeing how the love of God is at work in what we assume to be the "never-ending" punishment being expressed toward the goats.

Let's look deeper at the two Greek words translated as eternal and punishment. You may want to return to section 2.4, God is Eternal, to review the Greek words translated eternal. The word in this passage is aionios[4] meaning an age or unspecified period of time that has some particular character or quality. The focus of the word is what is happening in that period of time, not the duration. The literal translation would be an "age characterized by life" and an "age characterized by punishment." The sheep experience Aionios' life, and the goats experience aionios punishment.

A literal translation of aionios would be age life and age punishment. However, translating aionios as eternal in this passage is actually appropriate if we think of the character of life and punishment, not its duration. Unfortunately, when we read the word eternal, we think never-ending. But eternal describes God as existing outside of time. The idea is that what all mankind is experiencing is coming from the eternal. It is coming from God. It is not about the duration of life and punishment; it is about the quality of each of them.

Eternal life comes from outside of creation onto the sheep, and eternal punishment onto the goats. This passage has been used as a proof text for everlasting punishment. The logic goes like this: Since we know eternal life is forever, this passage proves that eternal punishment must also be forever.

But that misses the point the passage is communicating. This passage says that everyone will enter into an experience of the eternal nature of God at the end of this life. Those who possess faith experience life, and the rest experience punishment. The duration is unspecified. The point being emphasized is that the experience of both groups comes directly from an eternal God who exists outside of time and space.

---

4   aiónios - Strong's Greek 166 aiónios (an adjective, derived from 165 /aión ("an age, having a particular character and quality") – properly, "age-like" ("like-an-age"), i.e. an "age-characteristic" (the quality describing a particular age); (figuratively) the unique quality (reality) of God's life at work in the believer, i.e. as the Lord manifests His self-existent life (as it is in His sinless abode of heaven). "Eternal (166 /aiónios) life operates simultaneously outside of time, inside of time, and beyond time – i.e., what gives time its everlasting meaning for the believer through faith, yet is also time-independent. See 165 (aiōn).
[166 (aiónios) does not focus on the future per se, but rather on the quality of the age (165 / aión) it relates to. Thus, believers live in "eternal (166 /aiónios) life" right now, experiencing this quality of God's life now as a present possession. (Note the Gk present tense of having eternal life in Jn 3:36, 5:24, 6:47; cf. Ro 6:23.)] (Bible Hub)

Based on this passage and passages like it, we simply do not know the duration of the punishment coming to unrepentant people from God, who is eternal. What we do know is that it is motivated by all that God is, including His justice and His perfect love.

With that in mind, let's now look at the word kolasis, translated punishment in this passage. Our concept of punishment tends to have a more judicial, setting right the scales of justice tone. The following summary from Bible Hub describes the Greek meaning of kolasis:

Cognate: 2851 kólasis (from kolaphos, "a buffeting, a blow") – properly, punishment that "fits" (matches) the one punished (R. Trench); torment from living in the dread of upcoming judgment from shirking one's duty (cf. WS at 1 Jn 4:18). (Bible Hub)

Notice that this punishment involves a buffeting that is designed to "fit" or match the one being punished. It is individualized. Scripture teaches that some receive few blows and some many - Luke 12:47,48. The punishment that is received will be exact, motivated by agape and perfectly match what is best for the person being punished. The punishment also includes a sense of torment as the individual understands his accountability for his self-centered behavior. The punishment is not in any sense described as forever torture.

Since we know that punishment from God is motivated by His love, we are assured that it is being personalized for the good of the individual receiving the punishment. Based on an understanding of the nature of God and the original language used in the passage, it is my conclusion that the passage is not teaching that God is so offended by the goat's behavior that He chooses to continually, for all of the time, torture them to balance the scales of justice.

So, what happens to the goats? When they meet God, whose punishment is motivated by love, how will they respond? Unfortunately, the scripture leaves these specific questions unanswered. Are their hearts hardened forever in spite of God's love? Might they repent? Scripture introduces us to the judgment of God, but it seems to leave unanswered what, if anything, the judgment actually accomplishes.

I can be dogmatic about one thing. Those who experience God's judgment will be enveloped in the love of God while they experience the agony and torment of their choices that violated His love. They will be stopped dead in their tracks and have to face the horrors of what their sin has caused. Beyond this, I can only speculate. Might some repent? Possibly, but scripture is silent. If they did repent, would God forgive them? Based on His nature, it seems likely to me that he would, but again, the scripture is silent. What I do know is that God's love for them will never run cold and fail.

In the midst of the uncertainty, you can find confidence in this. If you know a friend or loved one who died in unbelief, while it is true that they are in a desperate situation, it is also true that they will meet the one who is forever the lover of their soul (Jn 3:16). However much you loved them, Jesus loves them infinitely more. Let that thought bring you hope!

Luke 6:36-38 (ESV)

36 Be merciful, even as your Father in Heaven is merciful. 37 Judge not, and you will not be judged; condemn not, and you will not be condemned; forgive, and you will be forgiven; 38 give, and it will be given to you. Good measure, pressed down, shaken together, running over, will be put in your lap. For with what measure you use it will be measured back to you.

Reflection:

Jesus is not providing a formula that we follow to receive His blessings. His point is that God's nature is merciful, non-judgmental, non-condemning, quick to forgive, selfless and generous. If we live our lives in the same manner, we are becoming like God, and His goodness flows into and through us.

Love is the one thing that grows by giving it away. It is the essence of kingdom living. When we give our love away with no thought of reward or blessing, our experience of God's love will return to us in abundance.

Set your eyes on His nature and bring into practice what you see in Him. It is in that place alone, where Jesus reveals more of Himself to us, that we experience eternal life.

Lord, grant me a heart devoted to love, generous, quick to forgive and not easily offended. May my attitude and responses always reflect your perfect nature, overflowing in abundance.

I Timothy 2:4 (ESV)

4 who desires all people to be saved and to come to the knowledge of the truth.

Reflection:

What a glorious affirmation of God's love for His creation. While this proclamation of truth is in perfect alignment with God's nature it does pose a number of theological questions.

If God desires all men to be saved, then why can't we assume that He will ultimately accomplish that desire? Are we so confident in our theology that we are certain God can't or won't fulfill His desire? Is God powerless to accomplish that desire because of man's free will, as the Arminians believe? Or does He have some greater desire that trumps this one, as the Calvinists believe? Or is the expression all people simply a reference to the Gentiles and does not actually mean all individual people? And if that is true, does it mean that God does not desire the salvation of all men? And so our theology rips to shreds what is otherwise a bold and beautiful declaration of the nature of God.

Are we willing to say man's free will is sovereign over God's desires? Or that His justice somehow trumps his love? Or that his love is two-tiered and He only longs for and seeks after the elect? Or will we protect the mystery of God's undivided, incorruptible nature?

I have trouble believing that God is unable or unwilling to fulfill what His love desires. That would require a perpetual conflict within His eternal nature. It is certainly true that God desires many things to change in our fallen world that are out of sync with His nature. But in the new creation, all things are perfectly reconciled to God (Col. 1:20). And while his desire continues unfulfilled in the corrupted universe, this world is passing and giving birth to a new creation that perfectly reflects the nature of God. Will God, in eternity future, continue to experience this unfulfilled desire? Will God allow evil to continually exist in the New Creation? If evil is forever punished then evil continues to exist.

Is this the reconciliation of all things? How do we so easily just accept such serious problems?

Our theological positions on judgment stand between us and what Peter has just revealed about God. I'm willing to allow God's nature to influence my thinking and challenge my theology of judgment if that theology mares God's glory in any way. Are you?

At this point, I need to address the elephant in the room. Am I a universalist? It is an ironic question, given the fact that I have become increasingly resistant to identifying with any form of systematic theology. When C.S. Lewis was asked if he was a universalist, he responded, "No, but I wouldn't be surprised if God was." That would be my response as well.

Lewis recognized an important idea. Thinking we have pigeonholed all the answers into a framework of theology and then organizing and labeling them can be dangerous. Yet, at the same time, he loved theological and philosophical discussions. It becomes a problem when we stop probing the mysteries of God and lock our minds into a fixed way of thinking. When that happens, theology becomes a straight jacket that limits our openness to where the Spirit of God may be leading us.

Peter tells us God's love is so encompassing that He desires the salvation of all mankind. May I encourage you not to wrap up statements like this in theological barbwire? Instead, ponder what this tells you about the goodness of our God.

God's goodness extends far beyond the limits of our theological understanding. Embrace the wonder of His infinite beauty.

James 1:20 (ESV)

20 For the anger of man does not produce the righteousness of God.

Reflection:

The Greek word for anger in this passage is the same word used to describe God's wrath in the gospels and throughout Paul's writings. James is making the point that man's anger and God's anger are nothing alike. When we get angry, we seek revenge; we want to settle the score. Man's anger is typically not motivated by love, and it does not produce anything righteous. But God's wrath is not vindictive in any sense.

God's wrath, unlike the wrath of men, does produce righteousness. God's anger is intended to make things right, not to settle a score with someone who has offended Him. When God pours out His wrath on sinners He is motivated by love and is always seeking to make things right. The idea that God's wrath is vindictive and occurs when His love is quenched, and He has finally lost His patience, is a serious violation of His revealed nature. His wrath is always motivated by love and intended to produce righteousness.

Allow your concept of God's judgment to be shaped by the knowledge of His perfect love. Based on what we know about God's nature, is it conceivable that God's love could react in a vindictive manner or that His love could shift in its nature from seeking what is best for the unrepentant into merciless, unending anger? My hope is that you can confidently say NO; God's nature is immutable. No amount of sin in all of creation will ever diminish His forbearing, enduring, never-failing love.

Exodus 9:12 (ESV)

12 But the LORD hardened Pharaoh's heart and he would not listen to Moses and Aaron, just as the LORD had said to Moses.

Reflection:

The LORD told Moses in Exodus 7:3 that He would harden Pharaoh's heart so He could execute all the plagues He had planned. This makes God sound terribly harsh. Did He plan to harden his heart so that He couldn't repent? Did demonstrating His wrath trump any love He might have for Pharaoh and the nation of Egypt? Why would He put Pharaoh in a situation where He was ready to surrender and then harden His heart to prevent it?

Would God do such a thing?

What is clear about the nature of God is that everything He does is just and motivated by His love. So right up front, it is certain that God's treatment of Pharaoh is absolutely just and motivated by perfect agape love. The passage must be understood through this lens. It requires a bit of digging to discern what is happening here.

The Hebrew word translated as hardened in Exodus 7:3 is qashah. Qashah means to be hard, severe or fierce. God told Moses that he would harden or make Pharaoh fiercely oppose Moses. Exodus 9:12 describes the way God accomplished this.

The Hebrew word translated as harden in Exodus 9:12 is chazaq. This word means to grow strong or to strengthen. It is translated in a wide variety of ways. Depending on the context, it can be translated as courageous, to become strong, to encourage, repair, harden, persuade, and prevail, to name just a few. God was strengthening or encouraging the Pharaoh. For what purpose did God strengthen the Pharaoh? The contextual reason appears to be that Pharaoh was ready to give up in the face of the horrific suffering from the plagues. But he wasn't giving up because He changed his view about God. He still believed in polytheism. He didn't reject his beliefs. He was simply beaten down to the point where he no longer wanted to defend them. But God's goal was not simply to get Pharaoh to submit. He wanted Egypt to recognize that He was the true God, not the pharaoh and his polytheistic religion. So, strengthening the pharaoh's resolve (hardening) to fight for his beliefs was an act of love that would relentlessly pursue the Egyptian people and break polytheism's grip over them. The purpose of the harsh judgment is revealed in Exodus 14:17,18:

<u>And I will harden (strengthen their resolve to fight for what they believed) the hearts of the Egyptians so that they shall go in after them, and I will get glory over Pharaoh and all his host, his chariots, and his horsemen. 18 And the Egyptians shall know that I am the Lord, when I have gotten glory over Pharaoh, his chariots, and his horsemen."</u>

The hardening was a strengthening by God to enable the Pharaoh to have the courage to keep fighting for his convictions. Love's goal was not for the Pharaoh to relent or submit; it was looking for the Pharaoh to believe in the one true God. The strengthening was a gift of God to help Pharaoh stay true to his convictions until he and the people of Egypt finally realized their polytheistic views were false and that the God of Israel was the one true God. That purpose of God, motivated by love, was fulfilled when the waters of the Red Sea fell in on the Egyptian army.

God actually told Moses He had two goals in Egypt. The first was to set His people free from bondage. The second was to show Egypt that Israel's God was the one true God. The hardening and the plagues were necessary for the second goal. Here is God's conversation with Moses in Exodus 7:4,5:

"Pharaoh will not listen to you. Then I will lay my hand on Egypt and bring my hosts, my people the children of Israel, out of the land of Egypt by great acts of judgment. 5 The Egyptians shall know that I am the Lord when I stretch out my hand against Egypt and bring out the people of Israel from among them."

Through the lens of God's nature, we discover that God's justice and love are being shown to Israel in their deliverance, and they are being shown to Egypt through suffering. God's plan for both nations was to move them closer to Him, and He loved them in different ways in order to accomplish that goal. Love always wins. Sometimes, it wins through grace, and at other times, it wins through wrath, but regardless of the means, God's love never fails.

Eph 1:11 (ESV)

11 In Him we have obtained an inheritance, having been predestined according to the purpose of Him who works all things according to the counsel of His will.

Reflection

All believers have obtained an inheritance that is predestined. Romans 8:29 tells us that we are "predestined to be conformed to the image of His Son." By adoption, we came into God's family and our inheritance as His child is to be made Christlike. Hebrews explains what this actually means: "He (Jesus) is the radiance of the glory of God and the exact imprint (image) of his (God) nature" Heb: 1,3 ESV. Our inheritance is His nature.

Just as Jesus bears the perfect nature of the Father, so shall we who love Him bear His perfect nature. That is the mind-blowing truth of who we are in Christ. Our inheritance is to perfectly reflect the nature of God to all creation. We were chosen, predestined, for this purpose. Our inheritance is not that we get what Jesus gets. It is far more glorious than that. Our inheritance is that we, in a sense, receive who Jesus is. His nature is our inheritance. When we see Him, we will be like Him (1 John 3:2,3).

When we focus our eyes on the nature of God we are focusing on our inheritance. As we do this, we begin to receive the inheritance in this life. It is like wealthy parents who lavish gifts on their children and grand children. The parents want their heirs to enjoy the goodness that they have laid up for them. But there will be a moment when it all becomes their inheritance. As we focus our eyes on His nature, we begin to enjoy the inheritance that He has laid up for us as believers.

May we keep our "Eyes on God" and enjoy the foretaste of promised things to come.

Colossians 2:2,3 (ESV)

... which is Christ, in whom are hidden all the treasures of wisdom and knowledge.

Reflection:

Wisdom and knowledge are the greatest treasures, and they are hidden. There is wisdom that comes from this world that is of some value, but comparing this world's wisdom to the wisdom hidden in Christ is like comparing costume jewelry to a diamond necklace. It may look good until it is set beside the real deal. Once you've seen what's real, anything else is a cheap substitute. Wisdom and understanding are hidden in Christ. They are found deep within the nature of God. They cannot be seen through any other lens than the nature of God. This wisdom comes from above (James 3:17,18) and is relationally found as we walk with Christ.

Lord, open my eyes that I may discern how your wisdom should be expressed in my life and all my relationships.

Ps 19:13 (ESV)

13 Keep back your servant also from presumptuous sins; let them not have dominion over me. Then I shall be innocent of great transgression.

Reflection:

There is a sin that we know is sin, and yet we find ourselves drawn to its lure. We have a presumptuous attitude that we can enjoy our sins and, at the same time, enjoy the goodness of God. But sin always takes over and begins to own us. It blinds us from seeing God's will and robs us of the relational blessings God desires for us. As Paul explained in Romans 7, it is not us but the desire of our flesh that draws us astray.

Lord, I am weak and easily drawn astray. Apart from you, I will fall into the snare of the evil one. Hid my soul in Christ, that Your goodness will protect me from my presumptuous sins.

Matthew 27:45,46 (ESV)

45 Now from the sixth hour there was darkness over all the land until the ninth hour. 46 And about the ninth hour Jesus cried out with a loud voice, saying, "Eli, Eli, lemn sabachthani?" that is, "My God, my God, why have you forsaken me?"

Reflection:

It's a common belief among Christians that God the Father turned away from Jesus on the cross. After all, isn't that what Jesus cried out in the moment of His greatest distress? Could the Father forsake Jesus in His hour of need? How is it possible that we could believe such a horrific thought? But you say, "Jesus himself said the Father had forsaken Him." That is correct. He did say those words. But do they reflect the perfect, ever-enduring, never-failing love of God for the Son? They do not! So, something else must be happening to Jesus on the cross.

Consider the context. Jesus is not only bearing the sin of all mankind; He is bearing in himself all the pain that we have endured because of sin. He is walking where we have walked. He not only bears our sin, He bears our grief and our sorrow and all the human feelings that flood our minds. He understands our greatest fears because He walked in all of them with us on the cross. Jesus is not describing a holy God whose hatred of sin is so great that He turned His back on Him in His hour of need. He is describing a love so great that it carries even our feelings of abandonment that are associated with our fallen human condition. Jesus is proclaiming how far love is willing to go to meet the needs of the human race.

Jesus has experienced our feelings of abandonment. Love never retreats from sin. The reverse is true. Sin always retreats from perfect love. If God feels distant from us, it is just that, a feeling, not a fact. God's love relentlessly pursues. We are the ones who run from God and fear that God has forsaken us. Jesus carried that fear for us on the cross. His perfect love has cast out that fear (I Jn 4:18). If God feels distant, we are the ones who have moved. On the cross, Jesus bore all the fear and pain of this human condition, including our fear of abandonment.

God does not turn His back on us. Never, under any circumstances, can we be separated from God's unfailing love. That fear was carried away by Jesus on the cross.

Ps 119:55 (ESV)

__55__ I remember your name in the night, O Lord, and keep your law.

Reflection

The night brings challenges to my heart and mind. In the silence of darkness, I begin to fear what the future might bring and the potential harm that could overwhelm me and those I love. But the thought of your name renews my hope in the darkness.

Remembering the Lord's name is to remember all that He is. In the night, when we focus our hearts on God's glorious nature, we are drawn closer to Him. In the morning, that intimacy with His goodness fills us with His energy to "keep His law" or, in modern vernacular, to "walk in love." We love because He first loved us. Meditate on His love in the silence of night so that you might grow in it during the light of day.

Eph 3:14-21 (ESV)

14 For this reason I bow my knees before the Father, 15 from whom every family in heaven and on earth is named, 16 that according to the riches of his glory he may grant you to be strengthened with power through his Spirit in your inner being, 17 so that Christ may dwell in your hearts through faith—that you, being rooted and grounded in love, 18 may have strength to comprehend with all the saints what is the breadth and length and height and depth, 19 and to know the love of Christ that surpasses knowledge, that you may be filled with all the fullness of God.

20 Now to him who is able to do far more abundantly than all that we ask or think, according to the power at work within us, 21 to him be glory in the church and in Christ Jesus throughout all generations, forever and ever. Amen

Reflection:

Paul prayed that believers might comprehend and experience the nature of God's love. We all begin the Christian life with an experience of God's saving grace at the cross. Through our faith, we are grounded and begin growing in Christ's love. While all believers have tasted God's love we all fail to see the limitless nature of His love. It is infinite, existing apart from creation, and it has no boundaries. In our humanness, we can't begin to fathom how boundless love would act in our fallen world. So Paul prays that we might have the spiritual power to begin to understand the unbounded nature of God's love.

Paul's prayer was not just that we understand love with our minds but that we also experience it. We can only share God's love with others to the extent we have personally experienced it ourselves. We cannot give away what we do not possess. The love we give cannot exceed the love we have received. And this ability to love is the very thing that empowers the gospel message. Jesus prayed to His Father for this love to be present in all believers in John 17:20-26, concluding His prayer in the following verse:

John 17:26 ESV - "I made known to them your name (nature), and I will continue to make it known, that the love with which you have loved me may be in them, and I in them."

Paul and Jesus were praying the same prayer. Our prayer should be that we, the children of God in this generation, might drink more deeply from the fountain of God's love and see it bubbling up from all the scriptures as we read them. This was Paul's desire for his generation as well and the thing for which he prayed. May we comprehend the nature of God as it really is as we focus our eyes on His self-revelation in scripture!

I Samuel 15:1-3 (ESV)

1 And Samuel said to Saul, "The Lord sent me to anoint you king over his people Israel; now therefore listen to the words of the Lord. 2 Thus says the Lord of hosts, 'I have noted what Amalek did to Israel in opposing them on the way when they came up out of Egypt. 3 Now go and strike Amalek and devote to destruction all that they have. Do not spare them, but kill both man and woman, child and infant, ox and sheep, camel and donkey.'"

Reflection:

In section 1.1, God's Character vs. His Actions, I promised to return to this passage in I Samuel and look for understanding based on God's nature. From a human perspective, the passage sounds like God is requiring Saul to commit genocide. It actually sounds like ethnic cleansing. He even requires Saul to slaughter little children and babies. God wants to obliterate these people.

As awful as this sounds, it's not the worst judgment we find in scripture. The Genesis flood, a direct act of God's judgment on sin, wiped out all but 8 people from the face of the earth. And the plagues prophesied in Revelations will destroy over half the human race. The harsh reality of God's judgment, not only in this life but the next, cannot be ignored. We must make a choice as we approach the subject of God's judgment. We can either look at these passages and bring God's nature into question. Or we can seek an understanding of the passages that are in harmony with what we know to be true about God. What will we choose? Will we look at God from man's fallen perspective, or will we look at Man from God's eternal perspective?

In addition to what we have already learned about God's nature, consider the following circumstances related to the Amorites:

1. God finds no pleasure in the death of the wicked (Ez 33:11). He finds no pleasure in what He has commanded Saul to do.
2. God prophesied to Abram that after the exodus of Israel from Egypt, there would be 4 generations until "the sin of the Amorites reached full measure" before He judged the Amorite's evil. What occurred in I Sam was God's judgment after 4 generations of opportunity to repent. (Gen 15:15,16)
3. Amalek attacked Israel unprovoked after crossing the Red Sea, and God vowed to blot them out from under heaven. (Ex 17:14)

The Amorites, undoubtedly inspired by Satan, were a threat to the fulfillment of God's redemptive plan for Israel and their role in bringing the messiah onto Earth. The Amorite nation was under the spell of the evil one. In fact, God granted them opportunities to repent for 4 generations, which they would not do. Their utter destruction would protect God's plan for redeeming mankind and reconciling creation to Himself. His actions were motivated by His love for the human race and His redemptive plan for them.

But what about the little children and the babies? Does that mean they were slaughtered and sent to hell? Or could it mean that in their death, God ransomed their eternal souls before Satan's plan corrupted another generation? We can only speculate. When God doesn't explain what He is doing, we must trust who He is. Remember, death in this life is not the worst fate that can befall us.

As hard as it is to understand, we must see that the horrific slaughter of the children had to be an act of love. Perfect love is fully present and motivates everything God does. Whatever the temporal and eternal fate of the Amorites happens to be, we can be certain that God's justice was also an act of love toward both the Amorites whom He was judging, the Israelites whom He was protecting and the human race that He was redeeming. He loved the Amorites with the same perfect love that He loved Israel and all humanity. God's judgment is never in conflict with perfect love, even when we are unable to reconcile the two.

There will come a day when this will all make perfect sense, and we will understand how the goodness of God is being fulfilled in His wrath. In fact, we will look at it, and our hearts will melt in amazement and adoration when we see the love of God at work motivating this horrific judgment. Then, we will wonder how we could have ever thought otherwise.

Conclusion:

As you read the Bible, allow your heart to search for the fullness of God's nature at work in the verses you are reading. Do this no matter how difficult the passage may seem or how long the process may take. It may take weeks, months or even years, but Jesus will bless that effort by giving you new glimpses into His relational love that you can bring into practice in your life. His Holy Spirit is the great counselor and comforter. Listen for His voice over the voices of human reason. He will reveal more of Jesus to you.

SECTION 6 - CONCLUSION

"a plan for the fullness of time, to unite all things in him, things in heaven and things on earth."

Ephesians 1:10 ESV

If you have managed to read this far I'd like to commend you for your perseverance. I've strived to share these ideas with enough explanation, examples and scriptural references to make them understandable. I have not tried to identify and refute all the possible objections. My intent is not to prove anything or change anyone's mind. My desire is that you, the reader, will be encouraged to place your hope entirely in the person and nature of Christ and not on your theological understanding of scripture or, even worse, your own personal musings.

Every system of theology ultimately falls short of the reality, which is Christ. They point to Christ. Some do so more faithfully than others. But each, in their own way, ultimately relies on human logic and reason. They take the truth past its boundaries and draw conclusions about God that are tainted by human reason.

My thesis has been that, at least to some degree, we can minimize this problem if we better understand God's nature and use that understanding as a filter when we read scripture. I've attempted to provide adequate insight into God's nature, plus examples of how this can influence our understanding of scripture. It can help us avoid thinking of God from a human perspective and creating a false image of him in our minds.

Remember this: God is 100% relational, scripture is 100% relational, and the plan of God is 100% relational. It is not about getting theology right and following a set of rules. It is getting love right and walking in it. Paul laid out the plan of God in Ephesians:

"a plan for the fullness of time, to **unite all things in Him, things in heaven and things on earth**"

Eph 1:10 (ESV)

This is the ultimate plan of God, a plan that will be accomplished in the fullness of time. Through all the suffering of this life and the curse of death, through the reality of evil and all the judgments on mankind, through the fire and brimstone and the lake of fire and through the agony of the cross and its victory over sin and death, the plan is and has always been this:

Everything in all of creation, both heaven and earth and all that is in them, will be brought into perfect relational unity in Jesus Christ, the savior of all mankind.

Paul described it like this in Colossians:

He is the image of the invisible God, the firstborn of all creation. For by him all things were created, in heaven and on earth, visible and invisible, whether thrones or dominions or rulers or authorities—all things were created through him and for him. And he is before all things, and in him all things hold together. And he is the head of the body, the church. He is the beginning, the firstborn from the dead, that in everything he might be preeminent. ***For in him all the fullness of God was pleased to dwell, and through him to reconcile to himself all things, whether on earth or in heaven, making peace by the blood of his cross.***

Col. 1:15-20 (ESV)

Christ himself is the plan. Perfect peace for all of creation, purchased by the blood of the cross, is the plan. The cross is a total victory of peace, reconciliation and unity for all of creation. The cross was a massive, nothing left behind, relational victory over a fallen creation. It is not a speculation. In the fullness of time the promise will be fulfilled in Christ.

It is on Jesus alone that we focus our eyes. With our Eyes On Him we will discover more of who He really is and participate in His plan to bring the victory of the cross to all of His creation.

Let's keep our EYES ON HIM, who is making all things new!   Rev.21:5

ABOUT THE AUTHOR

Martin's life journey was strongly influenced by a poignant statement from his mother. She would often say, "Never adopt someone else's opinion as your own. Think for yourself." Now, at the ripe young age of 72, this mindset has entrenched itself in all of His thought processes. He describes it as a blessing that influences every aspect of his life.

In his late 20's, Martin experienced a new birth in Christ. Since then, He has wrestled with many difficult questions about God that often seem unanswerable. His passion is to help others process these difficult questions and find a greater sense of peace in the midst of this life's doubts and storms.

www.ingramcontent.com/pod-product-compliance
Lightning Source LLC
Chambersburg PA
CBHW060331130626
46553CB00003B/966